"A Soldier-Like Way"

The Material Culture of the British Infantry 1751 ~ 1768

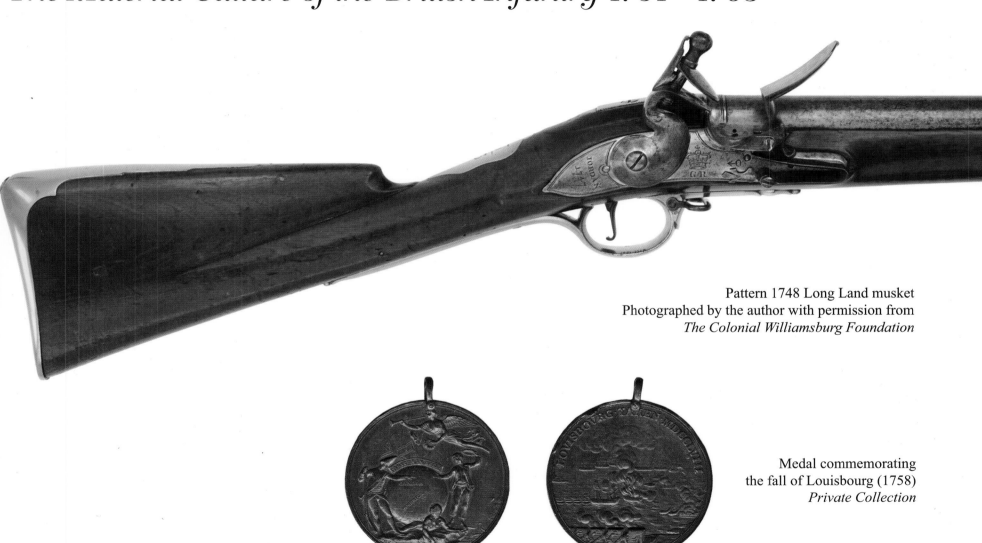

Pattern 1748 Long Land musket
Photographed by the author with permission from
The Colonial Williamsburg Foundation

Medal commemorating
the fall of Louisbourg (1758)
Private Collection

by R. R. Gale

Published in the United States by:

Track of the Wolf, Inc.
18308 Joplin Street N.W.
Elk River, MN 55330-1773
www.trackofthewolf.com

Tel: 763-633-2500
Fax: 763-633-2550

All correspondence concerning this book should be addressed to Track of the Wolf, Inc.

ISBN   978-0-9765797-2-4

Editors: John Neitz, Joshua Pollock

Cover: Front Background: *"A View of the Cathedral, Jesuits College, and Recollet Friars Church, taken from the Gate of the Governor's House."* Quebec, 1761. Richard Short.
Library and Archives Canada, Acc. No. 1989-283-7.
Foreground: 1756 Model Long Land Pattern Musket. *Private Collection.*
Miniature portrait of Lieutenant Parker Steele, 23rd Regiment, Royal Welsh Fusiliers.
Private collection.

Back: Infantry swords. *Private Collection.* 23rd Regiment sword (second from right) photographed with permission from *The Colonial Williamsburg Foundation.*

Contents

Foreword

Over the last century, countless military historians and collectors have written hundreds of books and articles on 18th -century material culture - the physical remains of the armies that carried out the military agendas of governments across the globe. Many of these works are very focused studies of the evolution of a narrow group of objects, usually weapons. Others are quite broad in their scope and include a seemingly endless variety of objects that might in some way have been associated with an 18th -century military camp. While all military material culture studies focus on objects and *how* they relate to an army, few have attempted to interpret the use of these objects *within* an army. At the same time each work is, in its own way, a commentary of the state of knowledge in a field of study, which historically, has received very little attention outside the historic arms collecting community. Individually, each is a benchmark in the evolution of military material culture research.

Material culture studies are not just about identifying historic objects and assigning them a date and place of origin, they are about understanding why objects are what they are and how they fit into an historic context. Good material culture studies rely on primary sources as the critical evidence that supports a framework of facts used to draw conclusions about an object. These are the types of studies that withstand the test of time. In this book, Ryan Gale has produced exactly this sort of work. He has scoured soldiers' journals, official military correspondence, military orderly books, and military manuals of all types to formulate this study. This approach has enabled him to use the army's own views on the materials it used on a daily basis to interpret the artifacts that survive today in public and private collections across America.

"A Soldier-Like Way" *The Material Culture of the British Infantry 1751-1768* is much more than its title suggests. It is not merely a book about guns and swords and associated "relics" of the British army. It is an analysis, a sort of object-based social history of the army's health and hygiene, clothing, garrison life and life aboard ship, and equipment differences associated with rank, responsibility and climate. The objects and art illustrated in this book compliment the information gleaned from period sources that tell the story of the life of a British soldier. The primary sources Ryan quotes are extensive, evocative and well footnoted.

With this work, Ryan has accomplished what many of us in the business of collecting, studying, and preserving 18th -century military objects have dreamt of doing for years - publish a concise material culture study that relies almost completely on primary sources to interpret the objects used by the British soldier in America. He clearly recognizes that weapons and accoutrements, uniforms and military insignia are not simply the tangible, often romanticized, remains of periods of intense military conflict in America's past. Ryan brings these objects to life by placing them in their proper military context within a well established and rigid military culture. For this he is to be commended because he addresses not only *what* is the material culture of the British army, but most critically *why* the army used the types of objects illustrated in this book. "A Soldier-Like Way" is *truly* a benchmark in military material culture research. It is a model for how military material culture studies should be approached today.

Christopher D. Fox
Curator of Collections
Fort Ticonderoga Museum
Ticonderoga, New York
July 2007

Preface

The actions of the British army during the period of the Seven Years War and Pontiac's Rebellion are well known, but the material culture of the soldiers who fought so bravely at Minden, Quebec, and Bushy Run has been relatively neglected compared to that of the more demonized and romanticized red coats of the American Revolution and Napoleonic Wars. This book examines the weapons, tools, food, and clothing that helped the infantrymen fight and survive under the conditions of mid 18th century warfare. There is an emphasis not only how these items were used, but how they were made, maintained, and eventually discarded. Though there is an emphasis on the British army in North America during the French and Indian War, the British army as a whole is addressed, at home and abroad, in wartime and in peacetime.

Very few complete uniforms from the 1750s and 1760s survive today. Clothing was only issued once a year, and was sometimes worn to tatters. When new clothing was issued, the previous clothing was often made into other useful items. Leather accouterments quickly deteriorated, leaving only the buckles and other metal parts. Weapons and metal clothing articles fared better due to the fact that they do not decompose as rapidly, and were often reused. Some items remained permanently locked away in the Royal Armories, others found themselves tucked away in attics, while others were left on the battlefields and campsites only to be recently unearthed. Many uniforms, weapons and accouterments still exist in the form of drawings and paintings created by artists and soldiers of the time. Journals, orderly books, and other records from the period provide futher clarification. My hope for this book is to shed new light on these objects by combining all of these resources into one reference, to bring the colonial British infantry studies into the 21st century by utilizing the most up-to-date tools and research, and to make the information available to the world.

Included in this book are a number of documents from the periods slightly before and after our target period of 1751-1768. These documents contain information regarding issues that are pertinent to this period. Text in italics with quotation marks are quotes from primary sources, and are left with their original spelling and punctuation. Artifacts are shown actual size where noted, and dimensions are provided whenever possible.

I would like to thank the following people for their contributions towards making this book possible: David and Carole Ripplinger, Erik Goldstein, Curator of Mechanical Arts and Numismatics, The Colonial Williamsburg Foundation, Christopher D. Fox, Curator, Fort Ticonderoga Museum, Karen Laweson, Colonel J. Craig Nannos, Martin West, Karl C. Smith, Larry and Jaye Beatty, Peter Donnelly, William P. Tatum III, John Neitz, Mark Tully, Barton Redmond Steven and Sally Nuckles, and Nicholas Hoffman.

Ryan R. Gale

2007

Introduction

The British infantryman evolved into the famous "red coat" between 1660 and 1700 under the monarchs of the House of Stuart. After the death of Queen Anne in 1714, in accordance to the Act of Settlement, the Protestant George I, Elector of Hanover, became King of Great Britain. Kings George I, II, and III reformed the British army on a scale never before seen. George I had a great interest in the military, being a soldier himself, and though he spent much of his reign in his beloved Hanover, he went to great lengths to improve the army that would be protecting his new kingdom. Among his most notable achievements was the creation of the Royal Regiment of Artillery, adopting a uniform drill exercise for the army, fixing prices for the sale of commissions, regulating stoppages, and improving the quality of supplies and arms.[1] King George II continued the reforms of his father, passing recruiting acts that offered bounties for enlistees, reducing the severity of military punishment, adopting standard patterns for all firearms, and established by Royal Warrant, a fixed clothing pattern for his entire army. In 1764, George III introduced his own drill manual, and a new clothing warrant in 1768.

Why did the Georgian kings pay such close attention to the management of their armies and the outward appearance of their soldiers? The king's army was a symbol of his grandeur and power, and thus the better the appearance of his soldiers, the more prestige it brought the monarch. The vast sums spent buying clothing and supplies from British merchants put money back into the nation's economy, and provided thousands of jobs. As a result, the country prospered. But most importantly, Kings George I and II lived in a time when kings still led their armies into battle, and thus much depended on their success, not only for the sake of their kingdoms, but also for their own lives. However, maintaining a well fed, equipped, and uniformed army in the mid 18th century was a difficult task, even for a kingdom as wealthy and as rich in resources and skilled leadership as Great Britain.

Grenadier, 13th Regiment of Foot, 1753
by William Baillie
Private Collection

"An Incident in the Rebellion of 1745" (Battle of Culloden), c. 1746
by David Morier
photographed by Antonia Reeve
The Royal Collection © 2007
Her Majesty Queen Elizabeth II

Weapons and Accouterments

The British army of the mid 18th century was divided into the English establishment and Irish establishment, each being maintained by their perspective parliaments and secretaries, and supplied by their own ordnance offices. In 1750, the peacetime standing army consisted of around 41,000 men, 17,000 of which were maintained on the Irish establishment. Since the troops were supplied and paid by the Irish Parliament, they lessened England's burden of supplies, and money.[2]

The standing army was granted to the king by consent of Parliament via the passing of the annual Mutiny Act. The king presided over the army as Commander-in-Chief, but because of his many duties of state he was authorized to transfer his military duties to a second in command, the Captain-General. Such was the case on March 6th, 1745, when George II appointed his son Prince William Augustus, Duke of Cumberland as captain-general of the army. In his twelve years as captain-general, Cumberland invented his own drill manual, created clothing guidelines, raised regiments of Scottish highlanders (a people he had previously suppressed), and he more than doubled the size of the army.

The backbone of the 18th century army was the infantry regiment. A regiment consisted of eight to ten companies of thirty to one hundred or more soldiers each. These numbers varied greatly depending on the establishment, the particular year, and war or peacetime needs. One company was made up of grenadiers, the tallest, strongest men in the regiment. The remaining soldiers made up the "battalion companies". In the late 1750s, one battalion company from each regiment was converted into a light infantry company, made up of soldiers who were agile and expert marksmen. A proprietary colonel commanded each regiment, with a lieutenant-colonel as second in command, and a major as third. The companies were commanded by captains, with the colonel, lieutenant-colonel, and major commanding the three senior companies.

In 1756, England was at war with France in what we now call the French and Indian War and Seven Years War. To meet this threat, Cumberland raised dozens of regiments and added additional battalions to existing ones, effectively doubling them in size. Thousands of soldiers were recruited from England, Ireland, Scotland, Wales, and the American colonies. Recruiting acts set down physical standards for recruits, which the officers were to obey:

"You are not to enlist any man under five feet four Inches High, or above the Age of thirty five years, or a papist, or a French Deserter. Your recruits must be broad shouldered, well limb'd and with out Infirmities, Ruptures, Scald heads, or sore legs".[3]

The British army used the volunteer system of recruiting. Recruiting parties from every regiment scoured the markets, hiring fairs, inns, and taverns throughout the empire enticing able bodied men to enlist with prospects of adventure, glory, and a cash bounty. When recruiting numbers were down, press gangs occasionally kidnapped men off the streets, and able men were plucked out of the militia.[4] The government issued each soldier with a basic stand of arms consisting of a musket, bayonet, cartridge box (now also known as a "belly box") with belt, leather bayonet frog and bayonet scabbard. Captain John Schlosser of the 60th Regiment writing to Colonel Henry Bouquet in April of 1764 described what was included in the stands of arms he received:

"…100 Stands of Arms Consisting in so many, Arms, Bayonets, Scabbarts, Steel Rammers, and Cartridge Boxes, are arrived…".[5]

The cartridge box was a simple block of wood with rows of holes drilled to hold cartridges, a black leather flap, and two leather belt loops. The belt loops were nailed to the wooden block with small iron nails on either the front or back side. The cartridge boxes of some regiments had flaps embossed with the king's cipher "GR" (Georgius Rex), while some regiments had undecorated flaps.

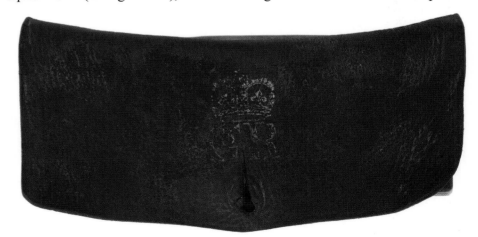

GR III marked cartridge box, c. 1760-1780
Courtesy Col. J. Craig Nannos

The cartridge box came with a black or buff leather belt with an iron or brass buckle. The simple sliding bayonet frog was constructed of two pieces of black leather sewn together and re-enforced with tinned iron rivets. A slot was cut into the front of the frog for the brass locket near the top of the bayonet scabbard to fit through, which secured it in place.

Right
Bayonet frog and scabbard
c. 1750-1780
Courtesy Col. J. Craig Nannos

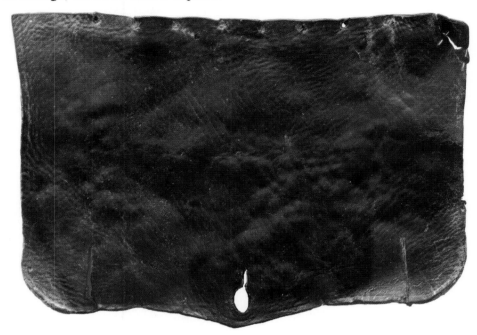

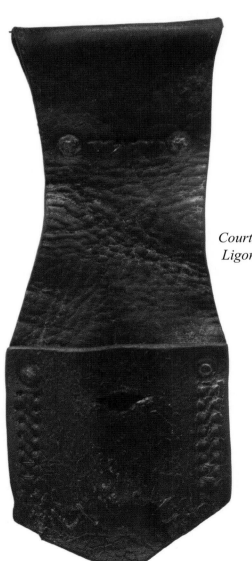

Left
Bayonet frog
c. 1758-1766
*Courtesy Fort Ligonier,
Ligonier, Pennsylvania*

Opposite
Grenadiers, 1st - 3rd Foot Guards, 1751
by David Morier
*The Royal Collection © 2007
Her Majesty Queen Elizabeth II*

Above
Cartridge box flap
c. 1758-1766
*Courtesy Fort Ligonier,
Ligonier, Pennsylvania*

Cartridge box
c.1760-1780
*Courtesy
Col. J. Craig Nannos*

1730 model Long Land pattern musket with wooden ramrod
Photographed by the author with permission from
The Colonial Williamsburg Foundation

Overall length: 62.95"
Barrel length: 46.00"
Caliber: 0.768

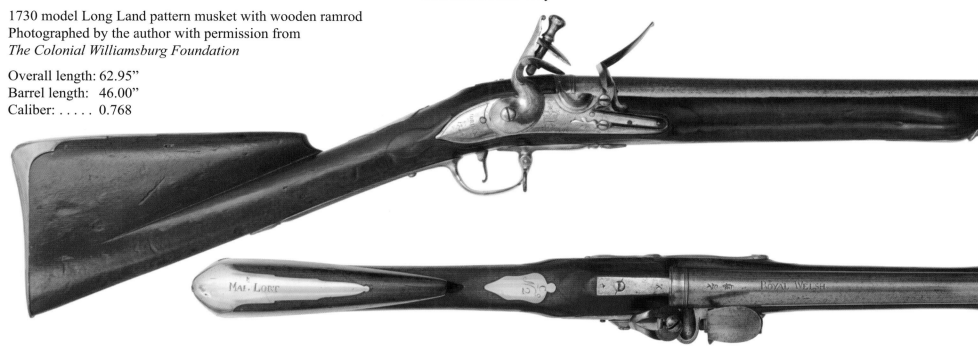

The Long Land pattern musket evolved between 1727 and 1760, and has been broken up into five distinct models: the 1730, 1730/40, 1742, 1748, and 1756 model.[10] The major evolutions between the 1730 and 1756 patterns were the addition of brass nose caps, external bridles, metal ramrods, smaller ramrod pipes, an elongated forward pipe, straighter lock plates, and stronger trigger guards.

The standard firearm of the British infantryman was the "King's" pattern or "Long Land" pattern flintlock musket, later nicknamed "Brown Bess".[6] The King's pattern musket made its first appearance around 1718, and was the first standardized musket in the British army. Before the Long Land pattern, muskets of varying sizes and appearances were purchased by individual regimental Colonels.[7] The Long Land pattern musket of the 1750s was a culmination of years of transformations, and improvements were continuing to be made until it was replaced by the Short Land pattern musket in 1768.[8]

The butt plate tang of this musket is engraved "MAJ[R.] LORT" signifying that it was issued to a soldier in the Major's Company.

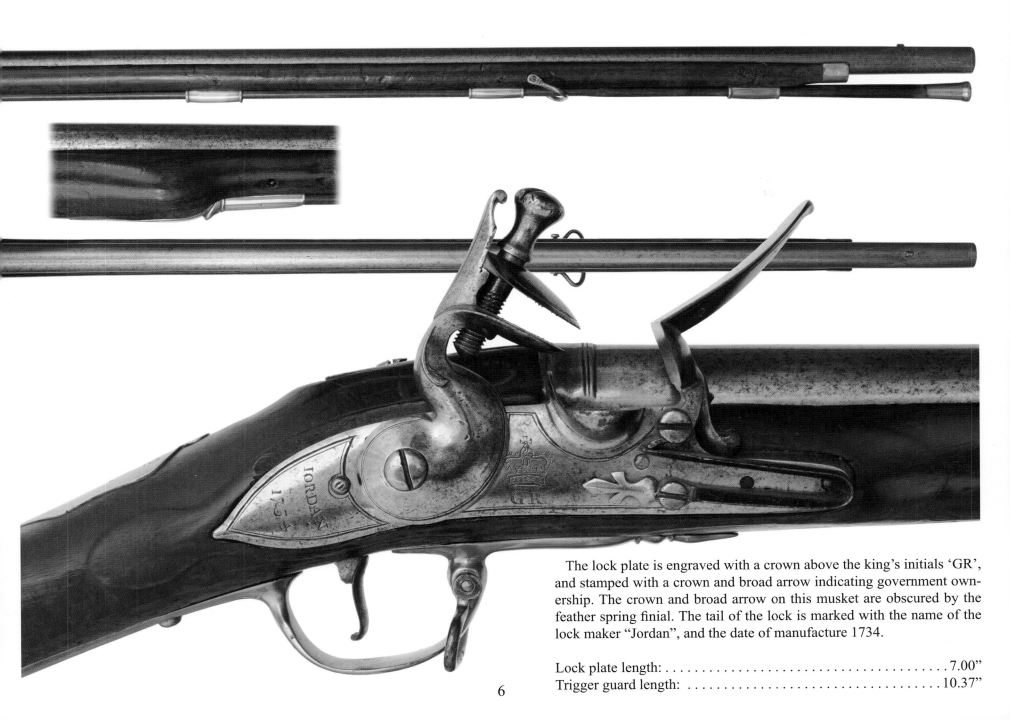

The lock plate is engraved with a crown above the king's initials 'GR', and stamped with a crown and broad arrow indicating government ownership. The crown and broad arrow on this musket are obscured by the feather spring finial. The tail of the lock is marked with the name of the lock maker "Jordan", and the date of manufacture 1734.

Lock plate length: . . . . .7.00"
Trigger guard length: . . . . .10.37"

6

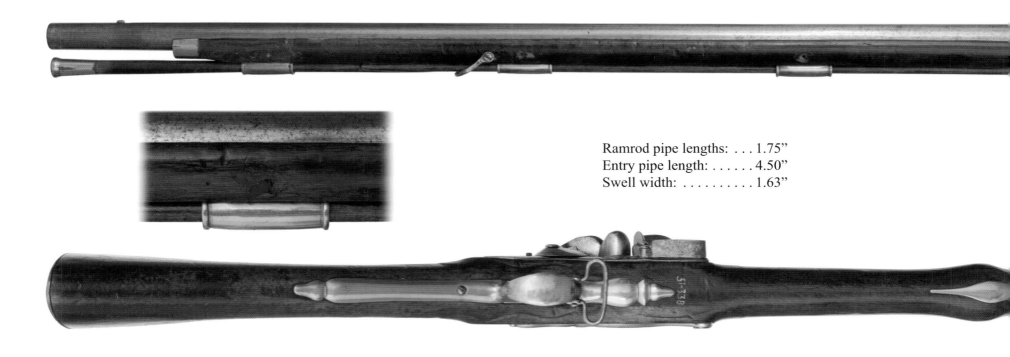

Ramrod pipe lengths: . . . 1.75"
Entry pipe length: . . . . . . 4.50"
Swell width: . . . . 1.63"

The Long Land musket was stocked in walnut with a brass trigger guard, butt plate, side plate, and ramrod pipes. The 46 inch smoothbore barrel varied between .75 and .80 caliber, and was secured to the stock using metal pins which passed through lugs fixed on the bottom of the barrel.

Initially, Long Land pattern muskets were supplied with wooden ramrods, usually with formed brass tips. In the early 1720s, iron and steel ramrods began to be used. By the mid 1750s, metal ramrods were becoming standard issue.[9] Metal ramrods were stronger, and lasted longer than wood, but had their drawbacks as General Hawley of the 33rd Regiment noted in 1726:

"...for if they have not some alloy of steel they stand bent and cannot be returned. If they have the least too much steel, then they snap like glass; in wet weather or in a fog they rust and won't come out".[10]

Formed brass wooden ramrod tip c. 1730-1750 shown actual size
Collection of the Fort Ticonderoga Museum

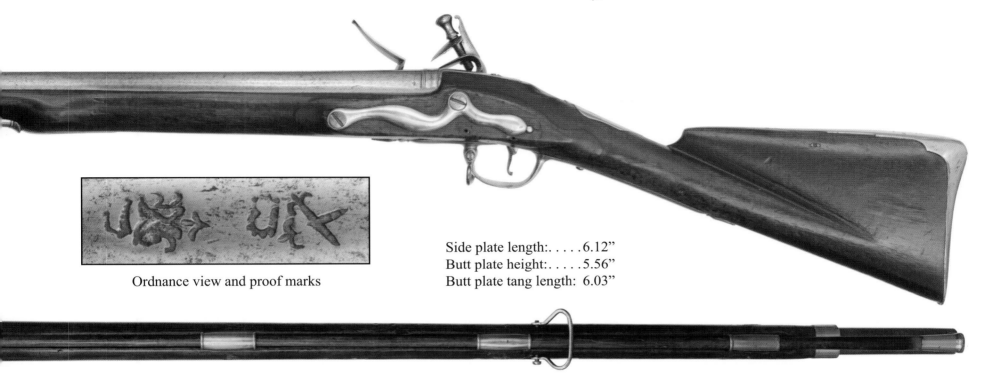

Ordnance view and proof marks

Side plate length:. . . . .6.12"
Butt plate height:. . . . .5.56"
Butt plate tang length: 6.03"

The barrel is engraved "Royal Welsh" signifying that the musket was issued to the 23rd Royal Welsh Fusiliers.

The sling swivels can fit a sling up to 1.6" wide.

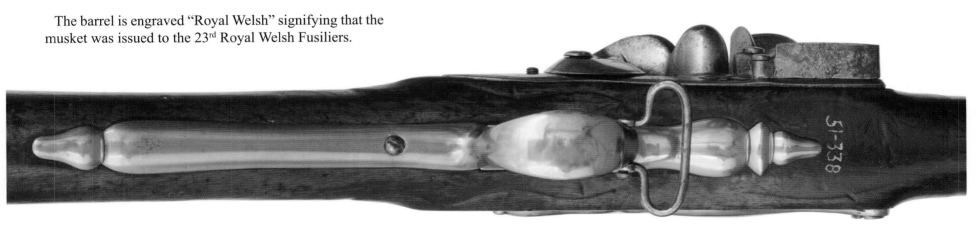

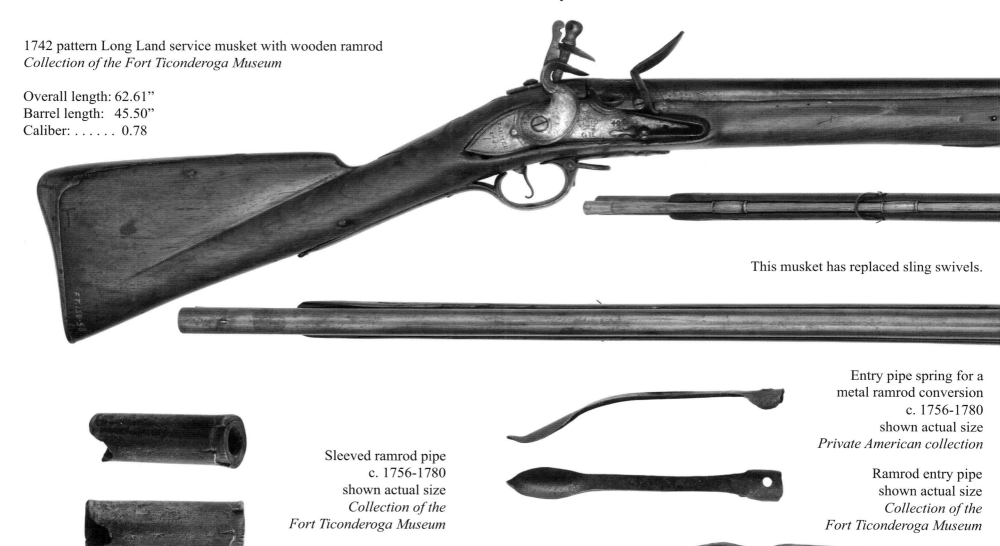

1742 pattern Long Land service musket with wooden ramrod
Collection of the Fort Ticonderoga Museum

Overall length: 62.61"
Barrel length: 45.50"
Caliber: 0.78

This musket has replaced sling swivels.

Sleeved ramrod pipe
c. 1756-1780
shown actual size
*Collection of the
Fort Ticonderoga Museum*

Entry pipe spring for a
metal ramrod conversion
c. 1756-1780
shown actual size
Private American collection

Ramrod entry pipe
shown actual size
*Collection of the
Fort Ticonderoga Museum*

When the conversion from a wooden to a metal ramrod was made, the pipes meant to hold the wooden ramrod had to be altered to fit the thinner metal one. To do this, a metal sleeve was placed inside the fore end pipe, and a steel spring attached to the inside of the entry pipe, which held the ramrod firmly in place.

Ramrod springs also had their drawbacks, as General Hawley observed:

"...the spring in the lower pipe is always wearing and breaking, and spoiling, by which they are a constant charge and tax upon the poor men as well as the rammers".[11]

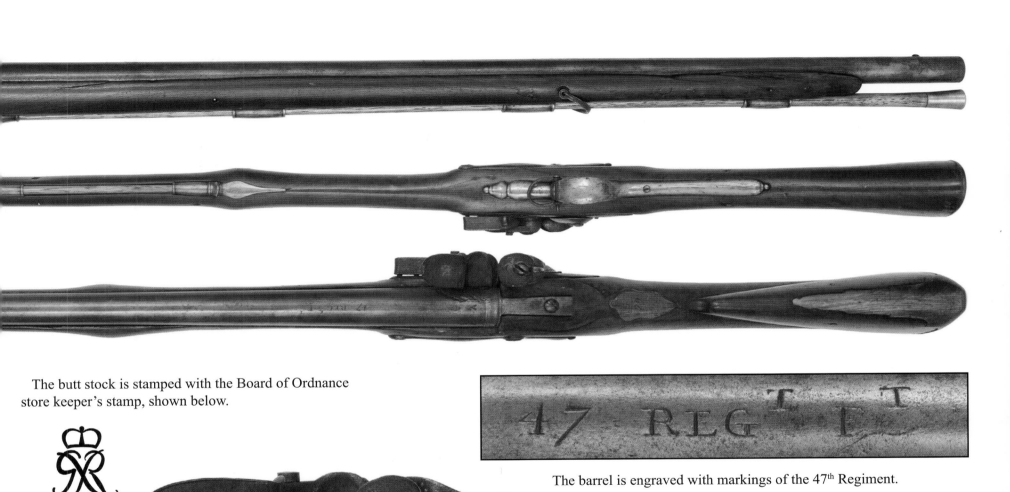

The butt stock is stamped with the Board of Ordnance store keeper's stamp, shown below.

The barrel is engraved with markings of the 47th Regiment.

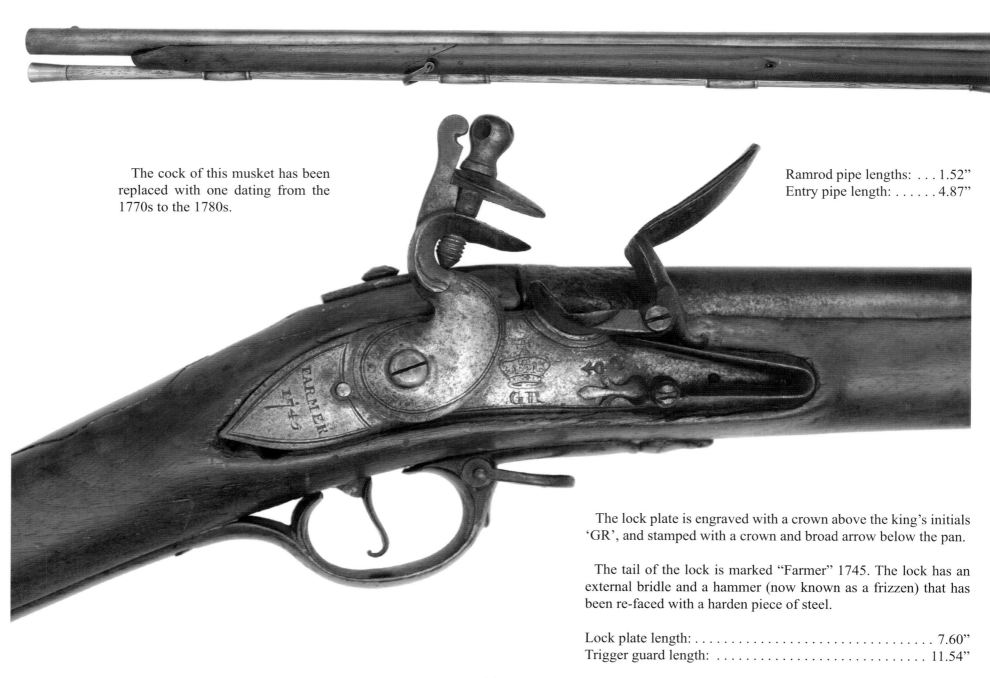

The cock of this musket has been replaced with one dating from the 1770s to the 1780s.

Ramrod pipe lengths: . . . 1.52"
Entry pipe length: . . . . . . 4.87"

The lock plate is engraved with a crown above the king's initials 'GR', and stamped with a crown and broad arrow below the pan.

The tail of the lock is marked "Farmer" 1745. The lock has an external bridle and a hammer (now known as a frizzen) that has been re-faced with a harden piece of steel.

Lock plate length: . . . . 7.60"
Trigger guard length: . . . . 11.54"

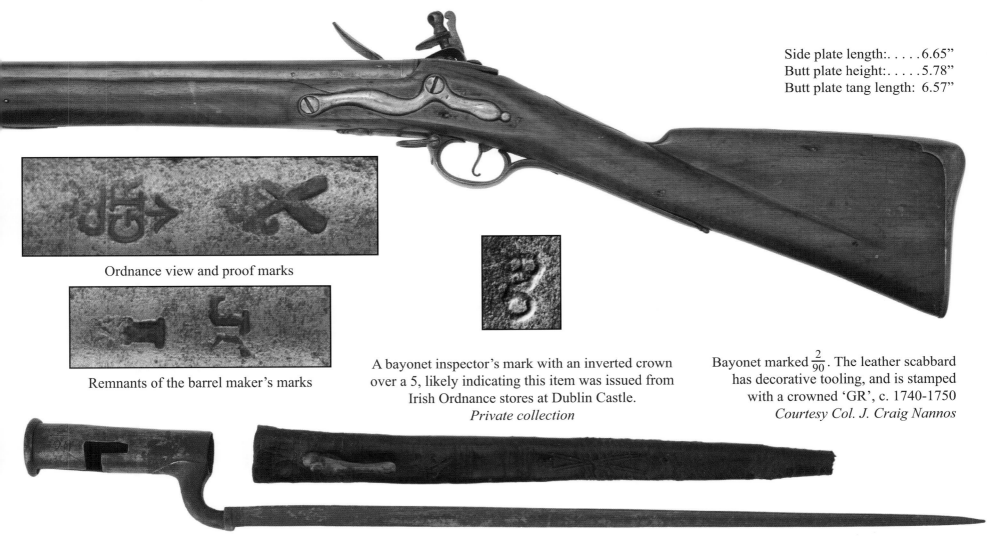

Side plate length:. . . . .6.65"
Butt plate height:. . . . .5.78"
Butt plate tang length: 6.57"

Ordnance view and proof marks

Remnants of the barrel maker's marks

A bayonet inspector's mark with an inverted crown over a 5, likely indicating this item was issued from Irish Ordnance stores at Dublin Castle.
Private collection

Bayonet marked $\frac{2}{90}$. The leather scabbard has decorative tooling, and is stamped with a crowned 'GR', c. 1740-1750
Courtesy Col. J. Craig Nannos

Every musket came with a well fitting socket bayonet. The bayonet had a triangular blade measuring around 17 inches long, with a 4 inch long socket, and came with a black leather scabbard. The scabbard was fitted with a cast brass finial at the tip to keep the point of the blade from poking through. A brass locket located near the top of the scabbard was used for securing it in the leather bayonet frog. When performing the manual exercise (musket drill), the bayonet was always to be wiped clean with a rag before being placed back in its scabbard.[12] Keeping the bayonet clean and dry kept it from rusting, and kept the leather scabbard from becoming wet and rotten from the inside.

Brass bayonet scabbard mounts
c. 1754
shown actual size
Jumonville, Braddock Road Preservation Association

Pattern 1748 Long Land musket with steel rammer
Photographed by the author with permission from
The Colonial Williamsburg Foundation

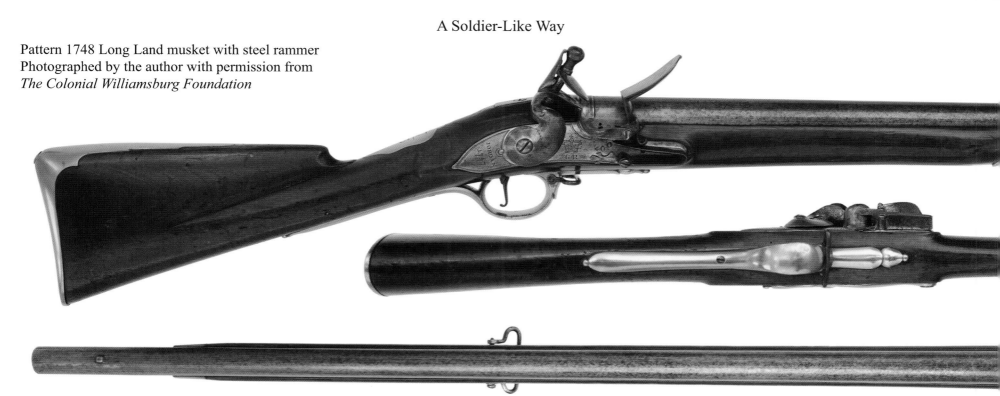

The Board of Ordnance was in charge of the construction and distribution of all firearms. The English and Irish establishments each had their own ordnance boards, independent of each other, headquartered at the Tower of London and Dublin Castle. Each board's staff included hundreds of master smiths, carpenters, wheelwrights, coopers, engravers, and laborers, all under the supervision of the master-general and his officers.[13] Components such as locks, stocks, barrels, and brass work, were contracted from suppliers throughout Britain and Ireland, shipped to the ordnance headquarters, and assembled into finished guns by royal armorers. This system of production was known as the "Ordnance System", and was first introduced in 1715.[14]

The Ordnance System was one way of regulating quality, and allowed the government to stockpile spare parts. Many of the parts came from Birmingham, where several predominant suppliers had workshops, which were often family owned and operated. Some companies made locks, while others forged barrels, cast brass parts, and cured wood for stocks. Many of the locks and brass parts were filed, stamped, or engraved with the maker's mark to indicate where they originated. As the barrels were being supplied by several different manufacturers, the Board of Ordnance, in an endeavor to regulate the quality, required proof tests and visual inspections of every barrel before purchasing them. A barrel

was first test fired with a lead ball, and three to four times the normal amount of gunpowder. The barrel was then visually inspected inside and out for damage. When approved, a proof mark and view mark (shown at right) were stamped on the top of the barrel near the breech.

Once the parts were collected, the weapons were constructed or "set-up" in a sort of assembly line. First, blacksmiths installed the underlugs and bayonet lugs on the barrels. Next, stock makers inlet the barrels, locks, and other hardware, carved the stocks, and did the final sanding and finishing. The stocks were stained with red, yellow, or brown dyes to achieve a uniform color, and finished with a varnish to preserve the wood. When finished, parts such as ramrod pipes, side plates, and individual lock pieces were marked with a number to indicate which firearm they belonged to.

Numbered ramrod pipes. c. 1750-1761. Shown actual size.
Collection of the Fort Ticonderoga Museum

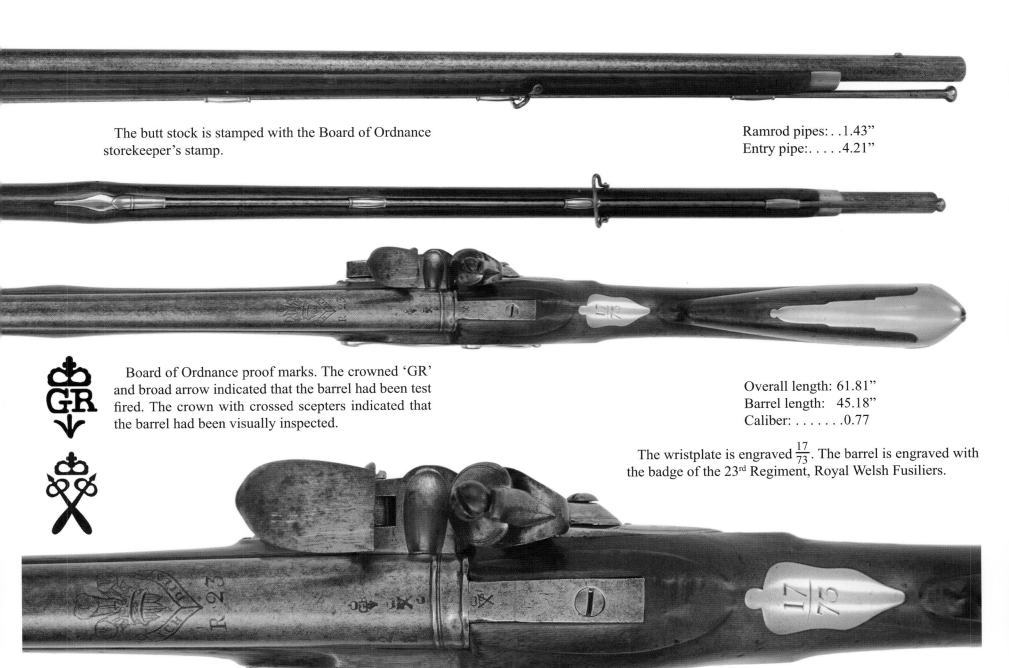

The butt stock is stamped with the Board of Ordnance storekeeper's stamp.

Ramrod pipes:. .1.43"
Entry pipe:. . . . .4.21"

Board of Ordnance proof marks. The crowned 'GR' and broad arrow indicated that the barrel had been test fired. The crown with crossed scepters indicated that the barrel had been visually inspected.

Overall length: 61.81"
Barrel length: 45.18"
Caliber: 0.77

The wristplate is engraved $\frac{17}{73}$. The barrel is engraved with the badge of the 23rd Regiment, Royal Welsh Fusiliers.

Rear sling swivel, c. 1754
shown actual size
*Jumonville, Braddock Road
Preservation Association*

The company and weapon numbers often engraved on a musket's wrist plate were sometimes engraved on the bayonet and ramrod to indicate which musket they went with.

The lock is marked 'JORDAN 1747'.
The pan has an external bridle.
Lock plate length: . . . . . 6.87"
Trigger guard length: 11.31"

Side plate length:. . . . .6.43"
Butt plate height:. . . . .5.12"
Butt plate tang length: 6.19"

Ordnance view and proof marks

Inspector's mark (left), and barrel maker's mark (right)

The musket wrist plate was often engraved with the number of the soldier it belonged to, the number of his regiment, and the number or letter of his company. Shown at right are examples of the 17th, 27th, and 50th Regiments. Notice the maker's mark on the back view, and Roman Numerals to indicate which musket it belonged to.

The armories at the Tower and Dublin Castle strove to always maintain a surplus of arms for home defense and for raising new regiments. In 1757, the Board ordered that the armory at the Tower of London should maintain the following arms:

     50,000 Long Land muskets
     10,000 Short Land Dragoon muskets
     50,000 Short Land muskets for Marines & Militia
     50,000 carbines for Artillery & Highlanders
     2,000 pairs of Land Service pistols
     20,000 Sea Service muskets
     10,000 pairs of Sea Service pistols [15]

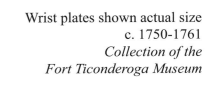

Wrist plates shown actual size
c. 1750-1761
Collection of the
Fort Ticonderoga Museum

1756 model Long Land pattern musket with steel ramrod
Courtesy Col. J. Craig Nannos

Overall length: 62.00"
Barrel length: 45.40"
Caliber: 0.80

Butt plate height:. . . . . 5.58"
Butt plate tang length:. . . . . . 5.80"
Side plate length:. . . . . 6.59"
Ramrod forward pipe length: 3.87"
Middle pipe length:. . . . . 1.40"
Entry pipe length: . . . . 4.66"

The lock plate is marked 'HASKINS 1758'.
The lock has an external bridle, a re-faced hammer,
and a replaced top jaw screw.
Lock plate length: . . . . 7.46"
Trigger guard length: 11.48"

This musket is stamped with a 'II PR' on the butt stock. The meaning of this mark is unknown.

The ramrod pipes of this musket are smaller in size to accommodate a steel ramrod. The forward pipe is elongated, tapered and trumpeted.

The sling swivels have been replaced with those from a later period musket.

Early 18th century Dutch musket, c. 1730
Photographed by the author with permission from
The Colonial Williamsburg Foundation

Butt plate height:.... 5.54"
Butt plate tang length: 6.91"
Ramrod pipe length: 1.58"
Entry pipe length: ... 4.57"

Overall length: 61.23"
Barrel length: 44.00"
Caliber: 0.81

It was customary for the ordnance office to issue older model muskets first. Only once these muskets were depleted would they issue new model muskets.[16] Muskets issued from the ordnance stores had the number or badge of the regiment they were being issued to engraved on the barrel to identify which regiment they belonged to. Even at full production capacity, the Board of Ordnance simply could not produce enough weapons to meet the needs of the military. To help meet the demand, the Board of Ordnance imported Dutch, Belgian, and other foreign made muskets, as well as barrels and other parts by the thousands. Dutch made muskets were the most common, and though slightly similar in appearance to the British Long Land pattern, were of lesser quality, and were reserved primarily for use overseas.[17]

Early Dutch musket lock mark (top) and barrel marks (right), c. 1740
Collection of the
Fort Ticonderoga Museum

19

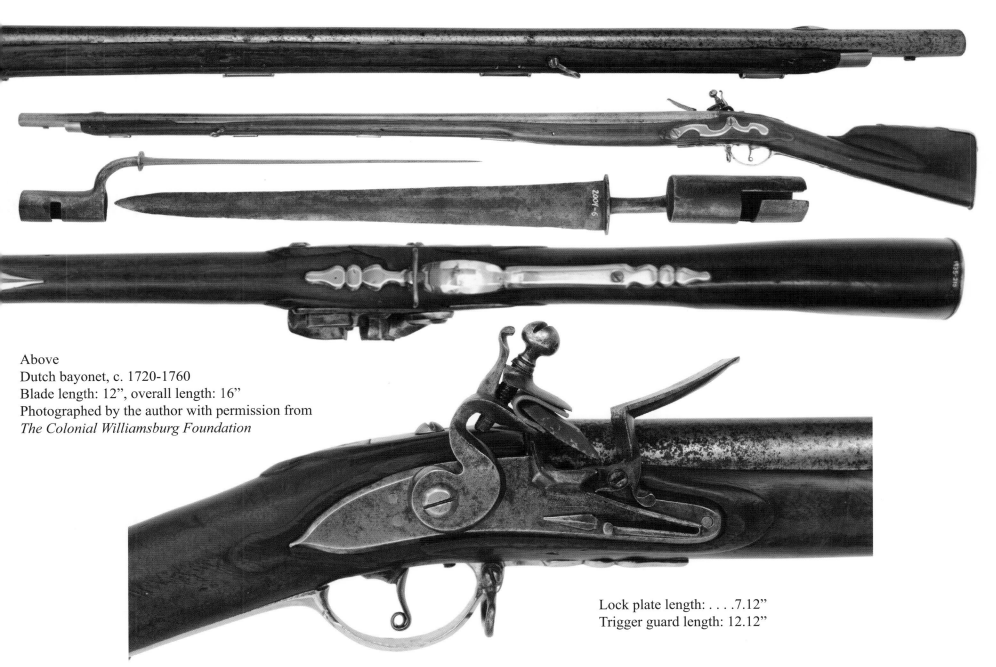

Above
Dutch bayonet, c. 1720-1760
Blade length: 12", overall length: 16"
Photographed by the author with permission from
The Colonial Williamsburg Foundation

Lock plate length: . . . .7.12"
Trigger guard length: 12.12"

Once the soldiers were issued their muskets, they were taught how to properly clean and care for them. As part of their equipment, every soldier was issued a turn-screw (screwdriver) for tightening the musket screws, a tin bottle for holding oil used to clean and lubricate the metalwork, an iron worm for swabbing out the barrel, a piece of buff leather for polishing the metal and brass, a wooden stopper for plugging the muzzle, a stiff hair pan brush, an iron vent pick, and a cloth wiping rag. Captain James Stewart of the 42nd Regiment gave the following order in February of 1760:

"The mens arms to be in perfect repair and to be completed in stoppers, pickers, brushes and hammer caps…".[18]

And in September of the following year:

"The arms to be perfectly clean without any grease, the brasses also to be well scoured and the firelocks to be rubbed again in the morning with a dry cloth… They are to carry their oil cloths for weeking their pans and bayonets".[19]

The musket barrel was cleaned by washing it out with water, and swabbing out the bore with a piece of rag or tow wrapped around an iron worm, which threaded to the end of the ramrod. The metal and brass work were always to be kept brightly polished. To accomplish this, wood ash, sand, or other abrasives were mixed with oil to create a gritty paste used to remove rust and polish metal. A final burnishing was done by rubbing the metal with a piece of buff leather.

After extensive use, the lock was removed and thoroughly cleaned. To protect the locks from rain, leather covers were sometimes provided. Captain Robert Stewart of the Virginia Regiment writing to George Washington in March of 1761 wrote:

"…the Nature of the Service we are likely to be employ'd in, will in some measure dispense with Bayonets, we can make Lock Covers of Cow Hides, and Hammer Slatts of Deer Skines &ca".[20]

Safety was an important issue. Accidental discharges were frequent, and occasionally resulted in the wounding or death of a fellow soldier, as General Jeffery Amherst noted in June of 1758:

"A man of mine wounded and one of Bragg's wounded by his firelock going off".[21]

As a safety precaution, a leather "hammer stall" or "thumb stall" was issued, which was placed over the hammer to prevent sparks should the flint strike it accidentally. Captain Robert Orme recorded in his journal on July 2nd, 1755:

"…an officer of a company is to see at retreat beating that the men fix on their thumb stalls".[22]

Musket tools
c. 1750-1780
Shown actual size
*Collection of the
Fort Ticonderoga Museum*

Threaded ramrod end
c. 1750-1780
shown actual size
*Courtesy
Col. J. Craig Nannos*

Iron musket worm
0.75 caliber, c. 1754
shown actual size
*Jumonville, Braddock Road
Preservation Association*

Morier's painting of the Coldstream and 3rd Foot Guards, seen on page three, shows dark brown covers on the hammers of their muskets, attached by matching straps. As an additional safety precaution, and to reduce wear on the gun flints, the flints were replaced with small pieces of wood for parade and drill exercises. Captain Stewart wrote in March of 1759:

"The men to have wooden flints in their pieces at exercise untill farther orders".[23]

When not on parade, on guard, or performing some other duty, the muskets were lodged in a conical tent called the "bell-of-arms", and were not to be removed without permission. On occasions when there were no bell-of-arms, or the soldiers could be expected to stand to arms at a moments notice, they were ordered to keep their muskets with them. Robert Orme recorded in his journal in July of 1755:

"No more bell tents are to be fixed: the men are to take their arms into their tents with them...".[24]

In a journal entry for June 29th, 1761, Corporal William Todd of the 12th Regiment recorded:

"...the Enemy remains tollerable quiet & we have Orders not to Uncannister but to Lay upon our Arms in our tents etc ready to turn out at the first Notice etc".[25]

Muskets constantly wore out or broke through vigorous use and exposure; thus the life expectancy of a musket was figured at about eight to ten years.[26] Each company was supplied with a number of replacement barrels, stocks, ramrods, and lock parts, to replace those that broke. The Board of Ordnance did not have enough armorers to accompany each regiment. Instead, the government issued money to the colonels to provide their own armorers or blacksmiths.[27] Most outposts and garrisons had a forge and tools which an armorer could use. Well supplied artillery trains often had a traveling forge and tools as well. A list of ordnance stores sent to America in 1754 included a *"Forge Cart complete with Anvil &ca".*[28]

In his orderly book for June 30th, 1758, Captain Alexander Moneypenny wrote:

"The Provincials to send their armourers & arms wanting repair to the artillery, where they will have use of the forge & tools".[29]

An armorer did minor adjustments and repairs to the muskets. The following prices for repairs were set by the quartermaster of Lord Loudoun's army in Halifax in July of 1757:

"Main spring – 1s   Hardning a hammer – 4d
Hammer spring – 8d   Caseing a hammer – 8d
Sear spring – 6d   New cock – 1s
Tumbler pin – 3d   New tumbler – 1s
New hammer – 1s   Swivel – 3d
*   Swivel pin – 2d"* [30]

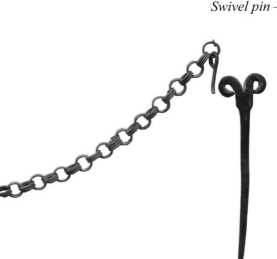

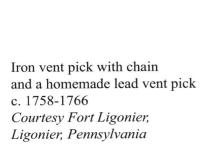

Iron vent pick with chain
and a homemade lead vent pick
c. 1758-1766
*Courtesy Fort Ligonier,
Ligonier, Pennsylvania*

Leather lock cover, c. 1758-1766
Courtesy Fort Ligonier,
Ligonier, Pennsylvania

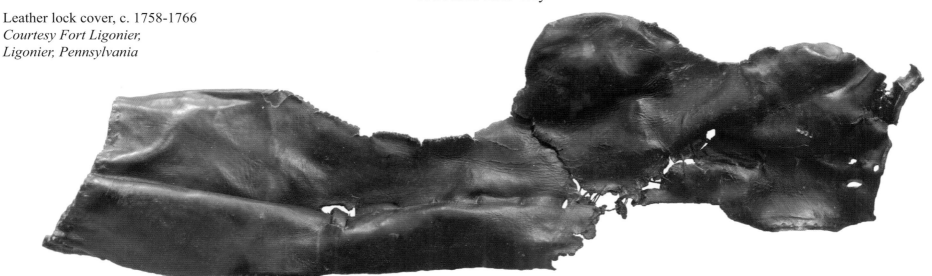

When any part of a soldier's musket broke, an inquiry was made as to whether it broke due to incompetence or accident; if the former, the cost of the repair or replacement would be taken from the offender's pay, and could possibly lead to punishment, if the latter, it was paid from regimental funds. Not only did the active duty soldier's firearms need to be maintained and mended, but also the arms of the dead, deserted, and discharged men, and the regiment's supply of spare parts. Captain Stewart wrote in his orderly book in March of 1759: *"The spare arms in the stores of the different Companys to be repaired with the outmost expeditions"*,[31] and Colonel Bouquet in January of 1764: *"The Spare Arms are to be cleaned & repaired and the Armourers are not to do any other work without a written order from Captain Hay"*.[32]

Soldiers depended greatly on their training, which could mean life or death in battle. Bravery was important as well, as cowardice could also mean death, either from the enemy, or by their own officers, as General Braddock stated in 1755:

"Any Soldier by leaving his company, or by words or Gestures expressing Fear shall suffer death and the Genl will greatly approve and properly reward those men who by their coolness and good Discipline treat the attempt of these Fellows with the contempt they deserve".[33]

The soldiers learned to march, maneuver, and drill with their muskets, first in small bodies, then as half companies, full companies, and finally as a whole battalion.[34]

They practiced the loading and firing sequence *"...first singly, then by files of 1, 2, 3, or more, then by ranks, and lastly by Platoons"*.[35] The men trained at least two hours, three times a week.[36] New recruits and "awkward men" drilled as often as twice a day or more as their officers saw fit. Captain Moneypenny recorded in his orderly book in July of 1758:

"The Regts under arms for exercise three times a week, choosing their own days, from six in the morning till eight in the front of their own encampment, to practice their men in loading & firing quickly, the recuits & awkward men of each regt to be out twice a day".[37]

Officers drilled their men indoors during the winter months whenever a suitable location could be found, which the case was for Colonel Samuel Bagshawe while in Cork in September of 1760:

"...I have secured a Market house for Drilling in, all the Winter".[38]

The soldiers practiced firing on different levels of ground,[39] and fought in mock battles to familiarize the men with the sounds and smells of combat as Captain John Knox of the 43rd Regiment recorded:

"A mock battle was arranged to aquint the soldiers to the nature of warfare in America,and to render the smell of Gunpowder more familier to the young soldiers".[40]

"A View of the Cathedral, Jesuits College, and Recollet Friars Church, taken from the Gate of the Governor's House." Quebec, 1761. Richard Short
Library and Archives Canada, Acc. No. 1989-283-7

Soldiers practiced firing at targets, which besides improving their accuracy, also *"teaches the soldiers to level incomparably, makes the recruits steady, and removes the foolish apprehension that seizes a young soldiers when they first load their arms with bullets"*.[41] Provincial officer John Hawks wrote in June of 1760:

"The recruits & awkward [squads] of ye regulars to practice with powder and ball at mark as often as the commanding officer of corps thinks it fit between the hours of 5 and 8 in the morning. They may likewise practice the Battalions at marks not exceeding 12 rounds per month".[42]

The targets were sometimes made of wood or paper as Captain Stewart described in April of 1759:

"All the shooting boards to be covered with papper and a black spot made in the middle".[43]

Other times, dirt filled gabions were used as targets, which allowed for the lead balls to be recovered:

"The regiments are out alternately, exercising and firing balls; for this purpose, stuffed gabions are fixed up for them, that the shot may be recovered, when ordered to be sought for".[44]

When ammunition was plentiful, the soldiers practiced firing several times a week. Occasionally, prizes were offered to encourage the men to do well, as in the 43rd Regiment in April of 1759:

"...the men are employed in firing at targets in which they are encouraged by presents from their officers, according to their several performances".[45]

Colonel Bouquet wrote the following request in the fall of 1764:

"Please to pay the above Men the premiums fixed in the public orders of the 20th Instant, viz three Dollars for the best shot, the next best Two Dollars, and four Dollars for the two next best shotts in Each Battn...".[46]

Target practice was far less prevalent in peacetime, as regiments were issued between 60 and 120 blank rounds per man a year, but only about two to four musket balls.[47]

Cartridges were made in Britain and shipped to regiments at home and abroad, or when needed, made in the field by the soldiers. A cartridge consisted of a tube of paper tied on one or both ends with thread, which contained a round lead ball and a measured amount of gunpowder. Gunpowder was manufactured almost entirely in privately owned mills in England and contracted for by the military. It wasn't until 1759 that the government began making its own gunpowder when it acquired the mills at Faversham.[48] Gunpowder was collected, proofed, and distributed from the royal laboratory at Woolwich, and the magazine at Greenwich.[49] Gunpowder was stored in wooden kegs with wood or copper hoops, which did not create sparks. According to the Board of Ordnance, a 100 pound keg was prepared with 80 ½ pounds of double refined saltpeter, 5 pounds of charcoal, and 4 ¼ pounds of brimstone (sulfur) each.[50]

Lead musket balls shown actual size, c. 1754
Jumonville, Braddock Road Preservation Association

Officials from the Board of Ordnance were often stationed with large garrisons, and occasionally followed armies on campaign. It was their responsibility to maintain and dispense ammunition. The Earl of Loudoun issued the following general order in July of 1757:

"The commanding offrs of ye different regts to send to Mr Furnis Contractor of ye Ordnance to Know what Time He will Appoint to Receive their Damaged Cartrages & Spare Bullets, for which He will Give a Recait".[51]

If no ordnance officials were available, the managing of ammunition usually fell to an officer of the Royal Artillery, as Captain Moneypenny recorded in June of 1758:

"One hundred men from the 42nd, 44th, & 55th Regts to be employed tomorrow in making cartridges, to parade at 8 oclock, & receive their directions from an officer of Artillery".[52]

Soldiers were only issued cartridges as needed. When they were no longer needed, any cartridges that were left were returned to the magazine.

When an officer needed cartridges for his men, he applied in writing to the officer in charge of the ordnance for the amount needed, as this general order in 1757 states:

"When Ever any Reg^t. Wants Ammunition, a Demand is to Be made in Writeing Sign'd By the Commanding Off^r of ye Reg^t. of ye Number of Cartragess Powder & Ball that is Wanted. - When & What Number of Cartrages they Lost, and How They Have Ben Expended".[53]

The soldier's cartridges were regularly inspected, and inquiries were made if any were missing. If a soldier wasted, lost, or sold his cartridges, he could be considered an embezzler of government property and charged three pence a piece, besides being punished:

"...Allso that we should Be Examind how maney Carthirigs we had & have an a Count took of how maney we had spent: & for the future Every man that shot a gun with out his Leave was to Be Brought Before a cort marshal & be delt with as an abuser of the Kings stores & find for Every Carterrig 3 pense...".[54]

If a loaded cartridge could not be drawn out of the barrel, the musket was fired in the presence of a non-commissioned officer in a safe area away from others, usually over a lake, stream, or swamp, where the affects of the ball could be seen, or into a dirt bank where the spent ball could be recovered:

"...ye Commanding off^rs of ye Sev^l Reg^ts May Send Such Men as Cannot Draw Their Charges to Fire them off In Presence of an Uncommishion.^d off^r, Who will Take Cair that their Men Fire Their Pieces Where No Accident May Happen".[55]

On campaign, it was not uncommon for cartridges to run out, or become damaged by the elements. When more cartridges needed to be made, the camp colour men, sergeants, or other soldiers were employed in making them. An officer was commonly present to make sure no powder was wasted.[56] Gunpowder, cartridge paper, twine, lead, molds, and ladles for casting balls were supplied by the Royal Artillery. When no artillery was present, each company could carry the necessaries for making its own cartridges. When gunpowder got wet, it could be restored by drying it in the sun, and mixing it with an equal quantity of good powder.[57] William Hervey wrote the following in August of 1760:

"The arms to be cleaned, ammunition to be examined, any that is damp must be laid out to dry, and if any cartridges are so spoiled as to be unfit for service, they are to be given in to the Artillery...".[58]

Besides the basic stand of arms, no other accouterments were issued by the government. Instead, the government provided regimental colonels with the funds to purchase items such as shoulder slung cartridge pouches, waistbelts, knapsacks, and swords. Because these items were purchase by the colonel, and not issued by the government, there was no standardized pattern. Thus, there were variations between regiments.

Cartridge pouches generally consisted of a black leather bag containing a wooden block drilled with rows of holes for holding cartridges, usually numbering thirty six, with a large black leather flap to protect the cartridges from the elements. A three or four piece shoulder strap made of buff leather measuring between 2 ¾ inches and 3 ½ inches wide was sewn to the pouch, and adjusted using brass or iron buckles.[59] The strap was worn over the left shoulder, with the pouch hanging over the right hip, and was secured to the shoulder by a strap and button sewn on the shoulder of the coat.

Ball mold
c. 1758-1766
*Courtesy Fort Ligonier,
Ligonier, Pennsylvania*

Cartridge pouch, c. 1750-1781
*Military & Historical Image Bank
www.historicalimagebank.com*

ROYAL REGᵗ

QUEENS REGᵗ

3 REGIMENT

Opposite
Grenadiers, 1ˢᵗ Royal, 2ⁿᵈ Queen's
and 3ʳᵈ Regiments of Foot, 1751
by David Morier
The Royal Collection © 2007
Her Majesty Queen Elizabeth II

Top
Brass cartridge pouch buckle
with two iron tongues, c. 1750-1780
shown actual size
Collection of the
Fort Ticonderoga Museum

"Major Chabbert Order'd the Quartermaster Serjeant with the Camp Color Men & me with the Pioneers to go into the Rear, up the Country and Search for some Yellow Clay & bring some, if we found any, for the men to Collour & Clean their Buff".[62]

To prevent one soldier's accouterments from being mixed with another's, each soldier's accouterments were marked with his initials or company number, typically on the back side. George Washington wrote the following to the officers of the Virginia Regiment in 1757:

"...no non-commissioned Officer or Soldier is ever provided with less than 3 good shirts, two pair of good Stockings, and one pair of Shoes, and that the initial letters of their names are marked upon their ammunition, clothes, and accouterments, which you must cause to be entered in a Book kept for that purpose, to prevent their swapping and changing their things".[63]

Grenadiers wore match cases on the front of their cartridge pouch straps. The match case was a tube of formed brass tapered to a point on one end (see page 132), with a turned wooden stopper on a brass chain. The wooden stopper was slotted to hold a piece of burning match cord which was used to ignite cast iron grenades. By the 1750s, Grenadiers were no longer carrying grenades, though they still wore the symbolic caps and match cases, and were occasionally still issued match cord, as this 1761 general order states:

Cuthbertson suggested the following in his 1768 work:

"To prevent the confusion and trouble that might arise by the men's changing their Accoutrements among each other, it is absolutely necessary, that the same figures, which are on the Soldier's Firelock, be also lightly stamped, with a hot iron marker, upon the inside of both his Belts and sling".[64]

A ledger from the 60ᵗʰ Regiment in 1759 included eleven shillings *"For a set of punches to stamp numbers"*,[65] which could have been used for marking leather accouterments.

"The CO's of regiments are immediately to order spontoons for the Officers who want them; Grenadier Officers fusees and bayonets / Match-cases and match for the Men to be provided".[60]

The waistbelt was made of leather matching that of the cartridge pouch strap measuring between 1 ¾ inches and 2 ¾ inches, and adjusted with a brass or iron buckle.[61] A leather frog was sewn to the belt on the left quarter, which held the bayonet and sword. To keep their leather accouterments clean, the soldiers were issued balls of clay colored to match their leather. Clay ball was mixed with oil or water and applied to the leather with a brush or cloth to cover stains. Corporal Todd wrote in his journal for June 23ʳᵈ, 1761:

A brass buckle similar in size
and shape to those used
on waist belts, c. 1750-1780
shown actual size
Collection of the
Fort Ticonderoga Museum

Iron hilted infantry hanger
with brass wire wrapped grip
c. 1750-1760
Blade length: 26.00"
Hilt length: 6.13"
Private collection

Infantry sword blade marks used by
Samuel Harvey of Birmingham, c. 1740-1760
Private collection

British musketeers had been carrying swords since before the English Civil War. But by the mid 18th century, the infantryman's sword had become more of a ceremonial piece than a functional one, often seen as more of a nuisance than they were worth, as General Hawley had realized twenty years earlier:

"tis soldierlike and graceful for the men to have swords, especially in garrison, but too many inconveniences attend them...they are a hindrance to them at their exercise, and a great one in marching, and a man having full enough to carry besides them. As to night parties, they make almost as much noise as the old bandoliers by rattling with the bayonet, and when are they ever used in the field or in action?".[66]

Except for those of the grenadiers and highlanders, the swords, or "hangers", were usually left in storage when the soldiers went into the field. Regardless, swords were issued to the troops until 1768. Many of the blades were made by cutlers in Birmingham, and measured between 22 and 31 inches long. The hilts differed from regiment to regiment, ranging from simple guards of brass or steel, to complex basket-hilts.

The army did not always receive the best or even adequate weapons and accouterments, as General Hawley stated:

"Those regiments which were forced to buy their new arms in Ireland are murdered if they don't change them. Those who bought their arms at Birmingham for cheapness are not much better".[67]

Sword blade markings, crescent moon and
three stars, c. 1730-1750
Private collection

"Dog's Head" type infantry hanger
c. 1740-1770
Private collection

Since many of the accouterments were privately purchased, the quality was up to the discretion of the colonel or his regimental agent. Regimental agents were contractors in charge of procuring clothing and accouterments for regiments, and acted as bankers between regiments and the Paymaster General. It was not uncommon for an enterprising colonel to take the money given to him by the government for buying weapons and accouterments, purchase cheaper substitutes, and pocket the difference. For example, the 88th Highland Regiment in 1761 was allowed £1 15s 7d per pair of pistols, and purchased poorer quality pistols in Birmingham for a mere 18 shillings a pair.[68]

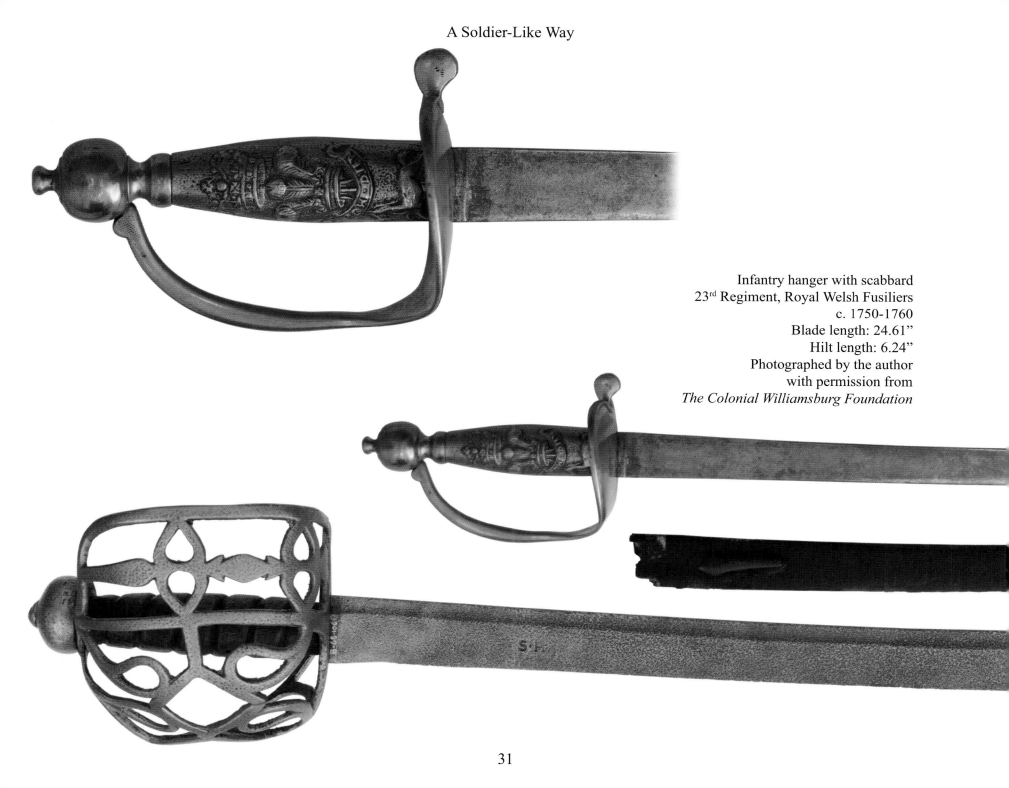

Infantry hanger with scabbard
23rd Regiment, Royal Welsh Fusiliers
c. 1750-1760
Blade length: 24.61"
Hilt length: 6.24"
Photographed by the author
with permission from
The Colonial Williamsburg Foundation

The *"fleur de lis"* an English maker's mark on the blade of an infantry hanger, c. 1750-1760
Private collection

Grenadier's half-basket brass hilted hanger as carried by the 1st "Royal Scots" Regiment
c. 1745-1760
Blade length: 30.50"
Hilt length: 5.63"
Private collection

The cartridge boxes and pouches belonging to William Shirley's 50th Regiment were drilled with holes too small to accept cartridges, and the leather was so bad that they fell apart on the march, as one officer explained to General Shirley:

"The holes of the pouches and boxes are so small that they cannot receive cartridges, nor is there substance of the wood to widen them sufficiently. The leather scanty and bad like wise".[69]

Since the accouterments sometimes came from more than one contractor, it was not uncommon for a regiment's belting, boxes, and weapons, to be of a variety of sizes and styles. The accouterments of the 33rd Regiment in May of 1754 were as follows:

"Cartouch-boxes all of different sizes, from 9 to 18 rounds...The Grenadiers' swords are of different kinds and unserviceable...The slings are all of different kinds, and a great many of them were made at Minorca in 1751, by Lieut.-General Johnson's orders, out of old rotton accoutrements...The black flaps are mostly peeled and cracked. The boxes in the pouches are mostly cracked and of various sizes, from 10 to 23 rounds... Breadth of the buffs: shoulder belts, some 3 ½ in., others 2 ¾ in. Waist-belts, some 2 ¾ in., others 1 ¾ ins. Slings, some 2 ⅛ in., other 1 ¼ in".[70]

It was common for regiments to transfer back and forth from the English to the Irish establishment. Whenever one did, the weapons from the old establishment were left in store, and weapons from the new establishment were drawn.[71] At the onset of peace, many regiments were reduced in strength or disbanded. The regiment's weapons and accouterments were returned to the Board of Ordnance, an inventory was taken, and the Board was compensated by the regiment for any missing or damaged pieces.[72] Any regimental markings on the firearms were removed by the armorers so they would be ready for re-issuing to another regiment in the future.

Left
Iron hilted infantry hanger with outboard branch and cast brass grip
c. 1750-1760
Private collection

Opposite
Grenadiers, 4th King's Own, 5th, and 6th Regiments, 1751
by David Morier
The Royal Collection © 2007 Her Majesty Queen Elizabeth II

KING'S
OWN REG.T

5
REGIMENT

6
REGIMENT

Clothing

With the assistance of the Duke of Cumberland and the Board of General Officers, the king issued a Royal Clothing Warrant on July 1st, 1751, setting down official guidelines for the uniforms of the army, from the color of each regiment's facings, to the emblems on their grenadier caps. Cumberland appears to have based at least some of the uniform articles set down in the warrant on the uniforms then being worn by his own regiment, the 1st Foot Guards.[73]

Brass coat button (top)
and waistcoat button (bottom)
c. 1750-1770
shown actual size
*Collection of the
Fort Ticonderoga Museum*

The uniform of
Captain Thomas Plumbe
1st Royal Lancashire Militia, 1760-1765
*Courtesy
King's Own Royal Regiment Museum
Lancaster*

The Royal Clothing Warrant, 1751[74]

George R

Regulations for the Colours, Clothing, etc., of the Marching Regiments of Foot, and for the uniform Clothing of the Cavalry, their Standards, Guidons, Banners, etc.

Our Will and Pleasure is That the following Regulations for the Colours, Clothing, etc. of Our Marching Regiments of Foot, and for the uniform Clothing of Our Cavalry, their Standards, Guidons, Banners, etc., be duly observed and put in execution, at such times as these particulars are, or shall be, furnished, viz., Regulation for the Colours, Clothing, etc., of the Marching Regiments of Foot.

No Colonel to put his Arms, Crest, Device, or Livery, on any part of the Appointments of the Regiment under his Command.

No part of the Clothing, or Ornaments of the Regiments to be altered after the following Regulations are put in execution but by Us, or Our Captain General's permission.

Colours

The King's, or first Colour of every Regiment, is to be the Great Union throughout.

The second Colour, to be the colour of the Facing of the Regiment with the Union in the upper Canton; except those Regiments which are faced with Red or White, whose Second Colour is to be the Red Cross of St. George in a White Field, and the Union in the Upper Canton.

In the Centre of each Colour is to be painted, or embroidered in Gold Roman Characters, the Number of the Rank of the Regiment, within a Wreath of Roses and Thistles, on the same Stalk, except those Regiments which are allowed to wear any Royal Devices, or ancient Badges, on whose Colours the Rank of the Regiment is to be painted towards the upper Corner.

The size of the Colours, and the length of the Pike, to be the same as those of the Royal Regiments of Foot Guards. The Cords and Tassels of all Colours to be crimson and gold mixed.

Drummers' Clothing

The Drummers of all the Royal Regiments are allowed to wear the Royal Livery, viz[t]. Red, lined, faced, and lapelled on the breast with blue, and laced with a Royal lace: The Drummers of all the other Regiments are to be clothed with the Colour of the Facing of their Regiments, lined, faced, and lapelled on the Breast with Red, and laced in such manner as the Colonel shall think fit for distinction sake, the Lace, however, being of the Colours of that on the Soldiers' coats.

Grenadiers' Caps

The front of the Grenadiers' Caps to be the same Colour as the facing of the Regiment, with the King's Cypher embroidered, and Crown over it; the little Flap to be Red, with the White Horse and Motto over it, "Nec aspera terrent"; the back part of the Cap to be Red; the turn-up to be the Colour of the Front, with the Number of the Regiment in the middle part behind. The Royal Regiments, and the Six Old Corps, differ from the fore-going Rule as specified hereafter.

Drums

The Front or forepart of the Drums to be painted with the Colour of the facing of the Regiment, with the King's Cypher and Crown, and the Number of the Regiment under it.

Bells of Arms

The Bell of Arms to be painted in the same manner.

Camp Colours

The Camp Colours to be Square, and of the Colour of the facing of the Regiment, with the Number of the Regiment upon them.

Devices and Badges of the Royal Regiments, and of the Six Old Corps

1st Regiment, or The Royal Regiment

In the Centre of their Colours, the King's Cypher, within the Circle of St. Andrew and Crown over it. In the three corners of the Second Colour, the Thistle and Crown. The Distinction of the Colours of the Second battalion is a flaming Ray of Gold descending from the upper corner of each Colour towards the centre. On the Grenadier Caps, the same Device, as in the centre of the Colours; White Horse and the King's Motto over it, on the little Flap. The Drums and Bells of Arms to have the same Device painted on them, with the Number or Rank of the Regiment under it.

2nd Regiment, or The Queen's Royal Regiment

In the centre of each Colour the Queen's Cypher on a Red Ground, within the Garter, and Crown over it. In the three corners of the Second Colour, the Lamb, being the ancient Badge of the Regiment. On the Grenadier Caps, the Queen's Cypher and Crown, as in the Colours; White Horse and Motto "Nec aspera terrent" on the Flap. The Drums and Bells of Arms to have the Queen's Cypher painted on them in the same manner, and the Rank of the Regiment underneath.

3rd Regiment, or The Buffs

In the centre of their Colours, the Dragon, being the ancient Badge, and the Rose and Crown in the Three corners of their Second Colour. On the Grenadier Caps the Dragon; White Horse and King's Motto on the Flap. The same Badge of the Dragon to be painted on their Drums and Bells of Arms, with the Rank of the Regiment underneath.

4th Regiment, or The King's Own Royal Regiment

In the centre of their Colours the King's Cypher on a Red ground within the Garter, and Crown over it: In the three corners of their Second Colour the Lion of England, being their ancient Badge. On the Grenadier Caps the King's Cypher, as on the Colours, and Crown over it; White Horse and Motto on the Flap. The Drums and Bells of Arms to have the King's Cypher painted on them, in the same manner, and the Rank of the Regiment underneath.

5th Regiment

In the centre of their Colours, St. George Killing the Dragon being their ancient Badge and in the three Corners of their Second Colour the Rose and Crown. On the Grenadier Caps, St. George Killing the Dragon; the White Horse and Motto "Nec aspera terrent" over it on the flap. The same Badge of St. George and the Dragon to be painted on their Drums, and Bells of Arms, with the Rank of the Regiment underneath.

6th Regiment

In the centre of their Colours, the Antelope, being their ancient Badge, and in the three corners of their Second Colour, the Rose and Crown. On the Grenadier Caps the Antelope, as in the Colours, White Horse and Motto on the Flap. The same Badge of the Antelope to be painted on their Drums and Bells of Arms, with the Rank of the Regiment underneath.

7th Regiment, or The Royal Fusiliers

In the centre of their Colours the Rose within the Garter, and Crown over it; the White Horse in the corners of the Second Colour. On the Grenadier Caps, the Rose within the Garter, and Crown, as in the Colours; White Horse and Motto over it "Nec aspera terrent" on the Flap. The same Device of the Rose within the Garter and Crown on their Drums and Bells of Arms, Rank of the Regiment underneath.

8th Regiment, or The King's Regiment

In the centre of their Colours the White Horse on a Red ground, within the Garter and Crown over it; In the three Corners of the Second Colour, the King's Cypher and Crown. On the Grenadier Caps, the White Horse as on the Colours the White Horse and Motto "Nec aspera terrent" on the Flap. The Same Device of the White Horse within the Garter, on the Drums and Bells of Arms; Rank of the Regiment underneath.

18th Regiment, or The Royal Irish

In the centre of their Colours, the Harp on a Blue field, and the Crown over it, and in the three Corners of their Second Colour, the Lion of Nassau, King William the Third's Arms. On the Grenadier Caps the Harp and Crown as on the Colours, White Horse and Motto on the Flap. The Harp and Crown to be painted in the same manner, on the Drums and Bells of Arms, with the Rank of the Regiment underneath.

21st Regiment, or The Royal North British Fusiliers

In the centre of their Colours, the Thistle within the Circle of St. Andrew, and Crown over it, and in the three corners of the Second Colour, the King's Cypher and Crown. On the Grenadier Caps the Thistle, as on the Colours; White Horse and Motto over it "Nec aspera terrent" on the Flap. On the Drums and Bells of Arms, the Thistle and Crown to be painted, as on the Colours, Rank of the Regiment underneath.

23rd Regiment, or The Royal Welch Fusiliers

In the centre of their Colours, the Device of the Prince of Wales, viz., three Feathers issuing out of the Prince's Coronet; In the three Corners of the Second Colour, the Badges of Edward the Black Prince, viz., Rising Sun, Red Dragon, and the three Feathers in the Coronet, Motto "Ich Dien." On the Grenadier Caps the Feathers as in the Colours, White Horse and Motto "Nec aspera terrent" on the Flap. The same Badge of the Three Feathers and Motto "Ich Dien" on the Drums and Bells of Arms; Rank of the Regiment underneath.

27th Regiment, or The Inniskilling Regiment

Allowed to wear in the centre of their Colours a Castle with three Turrets, St. George's Colours flying in a Blue Field, and the Name Inniskilling over it. On the Grenadier Caps, the Castle and Name, as on the Colours; White Horse and King's Motto on the Flap. The same Badge of the Castle and Name on the Drums and Bells of Arms, Rank of the Regiment underneath.

41st Regiment, or The Invalids

In the centre of their Colours, the Rose and Thistle, on a Red ground, within the Garter, and Crown over it; In the three Corners of the Second Colour, the King's Cypher and Crown. On the Grenadier Caps, Drums and Bells of Arms the same Device of the Rose and Thistle conjoined, within the Garter and Crown, as on the Colours.

Highland Regiment

The Grenadier of the Highland Regiment are allowed to wear Bearskin-Fur Caps, with the King's Cypher and Crown over it, on a Red ground in the Turn-up, or Flap.

General View of the Facings of the Several Marching Regiments of Foot

Colour of the facing	Rank and title of the regiments	Distinction in the same colour	Colour of the facing	Rank and title of the regiments	Distinction in the same colour
Blue	1st or Royal Regiment 4th or King's Own Regiment 7th or the Royal Fusiliers 8th or the King's Regiment 18th or the Royal Irish 21st or the Royal North British Fusiliers 23rd or the Royal Welch Fusiliers 41st or the Invalids		White	17th Regiment 32nd Regiment 43rd Regiment 47th Regiment	Greyish White
			Red	33rd Regiment (white linings)	
Green	2nd or Queen's Royal Regiment 5th Regiment Goslin Green 11th Regiment 19th Regiment 24th Regiment (lined with White) 36th Regiment 39th Regiment 45th Regiment 49th Regiment	Sea Green Full Green Yellowish Green Willow Green Grass Green Deep Green Full Green	Orange	35th Regiment	
			Yellow	6th Regiment 9th Regiment 10th Regiment 12th Regiment 13th Regiment 15th Regiment 16th Regiment 20th Regiment 25th Regiment 26th Regiment 28th Regiment 29th Regiment 30th Regiment 34th Regiment 37th Regiment 38th Regiment 44th Regiment 46th Regiment	Deep Yellow Bright Yellow Philemot Yellow Pale Yellow Deep Yellow Pale Yellow Bright Yellow Pale Yellow Bright Yellow
Buff	3rd Regiment or the Buffs 14th Regiment 22nd Regiment 27th or the Inniskilling Regt. 31st Regiment 40th Regiment 42nd Regiment 48th Regiment	Pale Buff	Red with Blue Coats	Royal Regiment of Artillery	

Abstract of the Foregoing

Blue . . . . 8 Regiments		Yellow . . . . 18 Regiments		Orange . . . . 1 Regiment	
Green . . . . 9 Regiments		White . . . . 4 Regiments		Blue with Red . . 1 Regiment	
Buff . . . . 8 Regiments		Red . . . . 1 Regiment		In all . . . . 50 Regiments	

When new regiments were raised, new warrants were issued laying down their official facing colors, lace patterns, and flags, like this 1758 warrant:[76]

> *6ᵗʰ November, 1758*   *Brown Street, Golden Square*
>
> *Sir,*
>
> *Inclosed is the Regulation for the facings, lace & c. of the fifteen Battalions which were drawn from the old Regiments, which be pleased to lay before the Clothing Board for their information. I am likewise order'd by his Excellency Field-Marshal Lord Ligonier to acquaint the Board, that the Battalion of Lord Forbes's which is order'd for the African Service, shou'd have Linnen Linings, Ticken Breeches, and Linnen Stockings as the Jamaica Corps have. His Lordship also directs me to acquaints the Board, that application having been made to him for permission to make the clothing of the Regiments serving in America without lace. His Lordship does not think himself at liberty to dispense with His Majesty's Orders, which Directs the Soldier's coats to be Laced, except the Regiment of Royal Americans, which from its first raising was permitted to be without lace, and Gage's Regiment of Light Infantry. I am*
>
> *Sir*
>
> *Your most obedient and most humble servant*
>
> *To Wᵐ· Fauquier Esqʳ·*   *Robᵗ· Napier, Adjᵗ· General*

With the look of each regiment's uniform fixed by royal warrant, it was left to the regiment's colonel, or his regimental agent to procure them. The first step was to contract with one or more clothiers to make the uniforms. Several merchants may have bid with the agent for the lucrative government contract. Given the instructions for the uniform's appearance, the tailors made a complete sample uniform, which was then submitted to the Clothing Board for approval.[76] The Clothing Board saw that the regimental clothing conformed to the royal warrant, and that it was of good quality. When approved, the clothing board sealed the pattern with a royal seal, and the tailors began contracting for their supplies of wool, linen, thread, lace, and other materials from various merchants.

Facings, Linings, Buttons and Lace proposed by the Colonels of the new Regiments, with the Regulation for their Second Colour, the First or King's Colour, being the Union with the Rank of the Regiment in the center, within a Wreath of Roses and Thistles.

	Colour of the facings	Colour of the lining	Buttons
61	Buff colour as the 3ʳᵈ	Buff	White
62	Yellowish Buff	Yellowish buff	Ditto
63	Very deep green	Buff	Ditto
64	Black	White	Ditto
65	White	White	Ditto
66	Yellowish Green as the 19ᵗʰ	Yellowish green	Ditto
67	Yellow as the 20ᵗʰ	Yellow	Ditto
68	Deep green	Deep green	Ditto
69	Willow green as the 24ᵗʰ	White	Ditto
70	Grey, but deeper than the 79ᵗʰ	White	Ditto
71	White	White	Ditto
72	Red	White	Ditto
73	Full green	Full green	Ditto
74	Green as the 36ᵗʰ	Green	Ditto
75	Red	Buff	Ditto
80	Dark Brown short coats	Dark Brown	Black

The woven wool cloth was produced mainly in the western counties of England where the famous Cotswold sheep and other long haired breeds were abundant.[77] Raw wool was also imported from Holland, Denmark, Germany, and Spain. The raw wool was spun into yarn and purchased by private weavers or large scale manufacturers. The cloth was woven on large wooden looms, thickened or "felled", washed, cropped, and pressed.[78] The process of turning raw wool into broad-cloth involved some thirty steps in all, and was generally an industry with very low wages. So prone were weavers to striking that the government was sometimes forced to regulate their wages.[79] In November of 1756, six companies of the 3ʳᵈ and 20ᵗʰ Regiments under James Wolfe were ordered to suppress a party of revolting weavers from Gloucestershire. Wolfe says of the weavers:

Lace	Drummer's Coats	Second Colour
White with a stripe of Blue	Buff	Buff colour Union in the upper canton, rank of the regiment on crimson in the center.
White, with 2 black & buff stripes	Buff	Ditto
White, green & white diagonal stripes	Very deep green	Deep green Union in the upper canton, rank of the regiment as before.
White, with one stripe of yellow	Black	St. George's Cross throughout, Union in the upper canton. Three other cantons black, rank of the regiment as before.
White, 2 stripes of deep yellow, blue & red & a blue worm	White	St. George's Cross throughout, Union in the upper canton, rank in the center.
White, with 2 crimson stripes	Yellowish green	Yellowish green, Union in the upper canton, rank in the center.
White, with one stripe of yellowish green	Yellow	Yellow, Union in canton, rank in the center.
White, 2 yellow & one black stripe	Deep green	Deep green, Union in the canton, rank in the center.
White, one red & yellow stripe, green worm	Willow green	Willow green, Union in the canton, rank in the center.
White, with a blue stripe	Grey	Deep grey, Union in the canton, rank in the center.
White, with 2 black and red stripes	White	St. George's Cross throughout, Union in the canton, rank in the center.
White, withe 2 red and one black stripes	Red	St. George's Cross throughout, Union in the canton, rank in the center.
White wth white, blue, & deep yellow, figur'd blue worm	Full green	Full green, Union in the canton, rank in the center.
White with 2 red and 1 yellow stripe	Green (for America linnen)	Green, Union in the canton, rank in the center.
White, with 2 green & 2 yellow stripes	Buff	St. George's Cross throughout, Union in the canton, rank in the center.
No lace	Brown	
By Order of His Excellency Field Marshal Lord Visount Ligonier Commander in Chief Robt Napier, Adj^t Genl		N.B. The Rank of the Regiment to be in gold characters on a crimson ground within a wreath of roses and thistles on the same stalk as the King's or first colour.

"They beg about the country for food, because they say the masters have beat down their wages too low to live upon, and I believe it is a just complaint".[80]

The woven wool cloth was purchased from the weavers by drapers, who dyed and sold the cloth by retail. A dull red dye was used for the private soldier's coats, made from the root of the madder plant, and a brilliant red dye for the commissioned officers and sergeants made from the cochineal insect imported from South America. Dyer's madder (Rubia Tinctorum) was cultivated to a small degree in Britain, but the majority was imported from abroad, particularly Holland, Denmark, and Spain, where the soil was better suited for growing madder plants.[81]

The dye was made by boiling the roots in a mixture of water, alum, cochineal, and other ingredients.[82] Dyeing was not an exact science. The wool cloth was dyed many times before the desired color was achieved, and the color varied between dye lots. The drapers sold the finished red wool to the tailors along with other colored wools required for making the uniforms.

Military clothing was often a reflection of popular civilian fashions, though Cuthbertson suggested that changes in fashion should "ever have but little influence, in making up the Cloathing of a Soldier, unless something occurs for the improvement of his appearance".[83]

ROYAL
FUZILEERS

KINGS
REGIMENT

9
REGIMENT

The coat or "regimental" of the mid 18th century infantryman was a well fitted garment, with turned back cuffs, lapels, small standing collars,[84] and skirts that could be hooked together with a hook-and-eye, or let down to protect the thighs. Coat designs differed for some regiments, such as those of highlanders and invalids. They will be discussed in detail later. The "facings", consisting of the lapels and cuffs, differed in color from regiment to regiment. The coat's interior and skirts were lined with wool, often in the same color as the regiment's facings, but sometimes in white or buff colored wool. For example, the Morier paintings show two regiments, the 33rd and the 24th, with linings of a different color than that of their facings. Likewise, the 1758 clothing warrant describes the 63rd, 64th, 69th, 70th, 72nd, and 75th Regiments as having non-matching linings and facings.[85] Sometimes linen was used to line coats, usually for those regiments intended to serve that year's campaign in a warm climate, as the letter written by Robert Napier on page 39 suggests.

Coat buttons (top)
and waistcoat buttons (bottom)
c. 1750-1770
shown actual size
Collection of the
Fort Ticonderoga Museum

Opposite
Grenadiers, 7th Royal Fusiliers, 8th King's
and 9th Regiments of Foot, 1751
by David Morier
The Royal Collection © 2007
Her Majesty Queen Elizabeth II

Hook-and-eye
c. 1758-1766
Courtesy Fort Ligonier,
Ligonier, Pennsylvania

To save time and effort, the lining was sewn together with each coat piece, instead of constructing the coat and lining separately and sewing the two together. The seams were then ironed flat and stitched to the liner. In some cases, coats were left unlined, like those issued to the Virginia Regiment in March of 1754:

"they were presented each with a suit made of thin, sleazy cloth without lining".[86]

The left shoulder of the coat had a strap with a button for securing the cartridge pouch to the shoulder. The coat's button holes and many of the seams were reinforced with worsted wool lace, usually decorated with woven patterns in a variety of colors, produced by merchant lace makers. Some regiments had plain white lace, while others had no lace at all. The lace patterns were chosen by the Clothing Board, but the shape of the laced loops was left up to the regiment's colonel.[87] The buttons supplied for the uniforms were either cast or formed from pewter or brass with hollow interiors. The shanks were made of metal wire, the tips of which were set into the back of the buttons during the manufacturing process. Buttons were not sewn on, but rather attached by leather thongs or cloth cords running through the shanks. Cuthbertson suggested leather should be used

rather than cloth to attach the buttons, as *"cloth ones will never hold them on"*.[88] Attaching the buttons in this fashion meant they could easily be removed and polished or replaced.

The coats were made in a sort of production line by a number of tailors, some cutting out the pieces, others working on sleeves, others on the body, while others sewed button holes and lace. The tailors did not make the coats in any particular size since regimental tailors would later alter the coats to perfectly fit the individual soldiers. It is possible that the tailors made a number of different sized uniforms utilizing a single pattern. Also, it is possible that certain seams were loosely stitched so they could easily be let out and altered later. According to Lieutenant Baillie of the 60th Regiment, a regimental coat weighed 5 ½ pounds.[89]

Besides the coats, the tailors also constructed the "small clothes" or "small mountings" which included breeches, waistcoats, gaiters, and shirts. The breeches were made of red wool, or blue wool for royal regiments. The legs of the breeches ended just below the knee, and were tightened at the base of the leg with a wool strap, buckle, and four buttons. Fall front and fly front breeches were both being used by the army and varied between regiments. The waistcoat was also made of the same red wool as the coat, lined with linen, and closed with ten or more metal buttons. The waistcoat had two small pockets, which may have been functional or not, with buttons or without, depending on the taste and finances of the colonel. Likewise, the colonel may have paid extra money for sleeved waistcoats. Like the coat, the seams of the waistcoat were reinforced with regimental lace. In some cases, linen small clothes were made for warm weather wear, and flannel under waistcoats for cold weather.

Captain Orme wrote the following in his journal in June of 1755 while marching with Braddock's army against Fort Duquesne:

"The soldiers were ordered to be furnished with one new spare shirt, one new pair of stockings, and one new pair of shoes; and Osnabrig waistcoat and breeches were provided for them, as the excessive heat would have made the others insupportable".[90]

In December of 1758, Knox recorded:

"The Colonel is orderd to provide the Regiment with flannel under-waistcoats…".[91]

Like the coats, the small clothes were not made in any particular size, since regimental tailors would later alter them to fit the individual soldiers. Breeches and waistcoat buttons were identical to those of the coat, only smaller.

Cloth gaiters covered the tops of the shoes and ended half way up the thigh. Gaiters were worn to protect the legs from brush, insects, the elements, and to prevent dirt and rocks from getting into the shoes. Gaiters were constructed from two pieces of heavy linen, sewn together with a single seam along the back of the leg, with a round extension sewn at the base to protect the shoe buckles. A leather or cloth strap buttoned under the sole to keep the shoe from falling off. Gaiters were painted or dyed a variety of colors. White gaiters were worn for parade, while black gaiters were for every day use. Brown and grey colored gaiters were also used. Cuthbertson suggested that grey gaiters were best if to be painted black.[92] Shank-less buttons made of black horn, wood, or metal closed the gaiters along the outside of the leg, numbering around thirty per leg. The gaiters were strapped to the leg just below the knee using black leather garters with brass or iron buckles. Major James Dalrymple of the 1st Regiment wrote in August of 1762:

"N.C.Os and soldiers not to appear in the streets without their black garters".[93]

Some regiments began adding leather tops to their gaiters as early as 1760 to prevent wear on their clothing, as mentioned by Colonel Bagshaw on October 3rd of that year:

"…I have ordered Tops of Leather to be put on the gaters when they go out to exercise & save the knees of Breeches & Stockings…".[94]

Knee garter buckle
c. 1758-1766
*Courtesy Fort Ligonier,
Ligonier, Pennsylvania*

One half of a brass
neckstock clasp
shown actual size
c. 1750-1781
Private collection

White linen gaiters belonging to
Captain Thomas Plumbe
1st Royal Lancashire Militia, 1760-1765
Courtesy King's Own Royal Regiment Museum, Lancaster

Breeches knee buckle
or garter buckle, iron, c. 1754
shown actual size
*Jumonville, Braddock Road
Preservation Association*

Neckstock buckle, brass
c. 1758-1766
*Courtesy Fort Ligonier,
Ligonier, Pennsylvania*

In 1762, those regiments fighting in Havana took to wearing ankle length spatterdashes, which were much cooler in the heat.[95]

Three to four shirts made of natural colored linen were issued to each soldier. The shirts had standing collars, which closed with a button of horn, bone, or wood, possibly covered with cloth. The shirts were made long, as was typical of men's shirts at the time, extending to the middle of the thigh, and acted as underwear. The shirts had simple ruffles at the breast about two inches in breadth. The cuffs were closed with metal or cloth cufflinks or buttons. Occasionally, shirts made of checked linen were issued, which may have been reserved for fatigue duty. The 42nd Highland Regiment received checked shirts in February of 1759:

"The Commanding Officers of Companys to provide their men furth with, with cheque shirts to the number returned wanting in each company".[96]

In 1749, the soldiers of the 20th Regiment serving in Scotland were not permitted to wear checked shirts as the cloth was too similar to tartan, which had been banned by the Disarming Act.[97]

A neck stock was worn around the neck, over the shirt collar. From looking at period drawings and paintings, rolling the shirt collar over the top of the neck stock was a common practice among officers, but less common among the rank and file. Cuthbertson suggested that the collar *"should not be allowed to turn over the stock, above an inch to prevent its being entirely hid".*[98]

Every soldier was to have two neck stocks, one made of black woven horsehair cloth, and one of finer white linen. The neck stock was adjusted at the back of the neck with a buckle or pair of clasps. Only one buckle or pair of clasps were issued per man, which were interchangeable between the two stocks.

The soldier's hats were made of thick black wool felt by merchant hatters, and were "cocked up" on three sides with black lace. The edges were bound with white wool braid. The hat was decorated on the right side with a Hanoverian cockade made of black woven horsehair cloth, which was fastened to the hat with black lace and a metal button.

These single hole bone buttons were probably covered with cloth and used on shirts or breeches
c. 1755-1780
shown actual size
*Collection of the
Fort Ticonderoga Museum*

Right
A detail from Morier's *"An Encampment of British Troops under the command of the Duke of Cumberland"*. The painting can be seen in its entirety on page 77.
*The Royal Collection © 2007
Her Majesty Queen Elizabeth II*

The shape of the hat sometimes differed from regiment to regiment. To maintain uniformity, the Duke of Cumberland issued the following order in 1751:

"H.R.H having observed that the hats of several regiments are cocked in different manners, is pleased to order that for the future all the hats of the Army be cocked in the same manner as those of the 1st Regiment of Foot Guards".[99]

The front of the hat was cocked with the front point over the left eye, the reason for which Cuthbertson explains:

"...this position of the hat, besides adding a becoming smartness to the air of a Soldier, places the left cock of it in such a direction as not to interfere with his firelock, in the motion of shouldering".[100]

Some regiments adopted the Hanoverian practice of decorating their hats with white cords with tasseled ends. These were wrapped around the crown of the hat, with a tassel hanging out each side. Amherst's 15th Foot was one such regiment:

"...The Hatts are cocked as you directed, & I have taken upon me to add a Hatband and Tassel à la Hanoverien. I think it gives the Soldier a good air...".[101]

The tall mitre caps worn by the grenadiers were made of stiffened felt covered with wool cloth and decoratively embroidered or appliquéd. The devices borne on the front of the caps were laid down by the Royal Clothing Warrant. Regiments with ancient badges displayed them on their grenadier caps, while those without badges were decorated with the royal cipher 'GR'. The emblem on the front of the cap was flanked by decorative scrollwork, sometimes adorned with floral sprigs. The back band of the cap was decorated with a lit grenade in the center, and the number of the regiment flanked by scrollwork. The top of the cap had a wool tuft matching the regimental colors. Though attractive, the tall caps were not very practical, as General Hawley explains:

"Our fashion of Grenadier caps are very handsome, but very inconvenient. A man suffers much in wet upon a march, and they are very heavy on a hot day, and the sun torments a man, and when they are sentry in cold weather".[102]

Two to four pairs of wool stockings and one to two pairs of shoes were contracted for each soldier. The stockings were to be knit, and not woven, though woven ones were possibly used when nothing else was available. Cuthbertson recommended that of the four pairs of stockings that each soldier should be is-

sued, three pairs should made of wool yarn, and one of fine linen thread for parade;[103] he also states that white was the preferred color for stockings, as it was the most *"showy"*, and was also the most readily available color, with grey being a suitable alternative.[104]

The shoes were made of black dyed leather with round toes and thick leather soles. The shoes were commonly made straight lasted, meaning they had neither a left nor a right foot. The shoes had no ties, but were buckled shut with oval or rectangular buckles. Cuthbertson noted that buckles and other brass hardware were found extremely cheap in Birmingham.[105]

Shoe with buckle
c. 1758-1766
*Courtesy Fort Ligonier,
Ligonier, Pennsylvania*

Brass shoe buckle
front and back views
c. 1750-1780
shown actual size
*Collection of the
Fort Ticonderoga Museum*

Opposite
Grenadiers, 10th, 11th and 12th
Regiments of Foot, 1751
by David Morier
*The Royal Collection © 2007
Her Majesty Queen Elizabeth II*

Besides making enough suits of clothing for the soldiers, a number of extra suits were made for each regiment to replace those that would be lost, stolen, or damaged, as well as uniforms for future recruits. Often, these extraordinary suits were simple lace-less frock coats. After the clothing was completed, an officer of the Clothing Board inspected them, making sure they were of good quality, and conformed to the sealed pattern.[106]

Large sums of money were required, not just to pay for the uniform and equipment needed for a regiment, but also to have it insured and delivered to the regiment, wherever it may have been stationed. An invoice of clothing shipped to America for the 55th Regiment in 1764 included (exclusive of damaged goods):

"455 pairs Breeches for soldiers
434 coats for ditto
438 shirts for ditto
483 cravats for ditto
466 pair stockings for ditto
548 hats ditto
48 coats for officers
35 shirts for ditto
39 cravats for ditto
39 pair stockings for ditto
31 laced hats
18 lb sewing thread, different colours
41 belts
36 thimbles
30 shoulder knotts".[107]

Rectangular brass shoe buckle
c. 1750-1780
shown actual size
Collection of the
Fort Ticonderoga Museum

It was the colonel's job to finance his regiment, either with his own money, or more often with government grants. The colonel or his agent determined how much money was needed to pay the tailors, hatters, shoemakers, and other suppliers, and submitted a request to the Paymaster General, who in turn passed it on to the Secretary-at-War, who presented it before the House of Commons for approval by Parliament. When approved, the money was issued back to the regiment's agent, often in installments.[108] Of a private soldier's daily wage of eight pence, two pence were deducted to repay the expense of his clothing and accouterments, among other things.[109]

The completed and inspected uniforms were insured and delivered into the hands of the regiment's quartermaster. The quartermaster, often one of the regiment's non-commissioned officers, was in charge of the regiment's supplies, tools, and materials. The yearly allotment of clothing was supposed to be issued to all soldiers on the 11th of June to celebrate the accession of George II to the throne, or the 22nd of September (after 1760) to celebrate the accession of George III.

"we are in great wants of our cloaths, as we have not reciev'd any this year yet, though they always should come against the 11th of June".[110]

"The King's pleasure is that the clothing for all regiments in America shall be delivered out every year on the 22d day of september, being the day of his Majesty's coronation".[111]

In some cases, a regiment's clothing took months to deliver. Regiments serving overseas fared the worst in this regard, as the long voyage may have taken several weeks or months, and the clothing was susceptible to being damaged, lost, or captured by the enemy. When a regiment received its clothing, it was the duty of its regimental tailors and their assistants to fit the uniforms to the individual soldiers. Regimental tailors were soldiers who had worked as tailors before joining the army, or soldiers who simply had some knowledge of sewing. Out of the 96 recruits raised by Provincial Captain Benjamin Noxon in 1758, five were recorded as having been tailors.[112]

In 1760, a sergeant major of the 60th Regiment was passed over for a promotion to ensign because his tailoring skills were too useful to the regiment.[113]

Tailor's shears
c. 1760-1780
Private American collection

If there were too few tailors, or none at all, some were brought in from outside the regiment, as in the case of the 12th Regiment in 1761:

"The Clothing goes fast on as all the Country Taylors is Employ'd that will work of all sorts".[114]

When their services were required, the tailors were billeted together and were free of any other duty until their job was finished. Part of the expenses of the 60th Regiment recorded in July of 1759 included £71 5s 11d for *"...Altering and fitting the Battalion cloathing by the Regiments Taylor, for a work room, fire and candles for them"*.[115]

Corporal Todd wrote in his journal on June 2nd, 1761:

"...all Taylors & Others that can be Assistant in making them up to fit the men are to be duty free & work upon the Cloathing".[116]

A head tailor was appointed to oversee the work, and that it was done according to the sealed pattern. Often, a guard was placed over the tailors to prevent them from stealing any materials, articles of clothing, and as Corporal William Todd explains, to *"not let any of the Taylors out to drink and Neglect their work"*,[117] though on the 6th of June, 1761, Todd recorded that five tailors *"receiv'd 100 Lashes each"* for doing just that.[118] Captain Stewart of the 42nd Regiment stated that the tailors of his company were to *"work from 7 o'clock in the morning till sunset allowing one hour for dinner. Such days as are not fit for exercise they are to begin their work at 5 o'clock in the morning"*.[119] With the amount of work required of them, it was not uncommon for the tailors to toil nearly all day and all night.[120]

The prices for altering clothing were set by a regimental officer. The major of the 12th Regiment in 1761 set the prices at eight pence per coat, eight pence per pair of breeches, and one shilling per waistcoat.[121] This money was used for paying the tailors extraordinary wages, and to pay for thread and other sewing supplies. In June of 1760, Captain Stewart recorded in his orderly book:

"It is Major Reids orders – the tailors at Fort Edward were payd one shilling sterling for making the waistcoats and one shilling currency for the other workers and obliged to find thread out of the shilling sterling to make the Regiments waistcoats".[122]

Steel needles, c. 1750-1780
shown actual size
*Collection of the
Fort Ticonderoga Museum*

The uniforms of the grenadier company were altered first, then the remaining companies according to seniority.[123] The condition of the men's old coats, waistcoats, and breeches dictated which of the three new articles would be altered first. The men in each company most in need of new clothing were given top priority.[124] The soldier's clothes were to be *"delivered out and fitted with great exactness"*.[125] The coats were pre-shrunk by dipping them in water and drying them in the sun.[126] Measurements were taken of the soldiers and the coats, particularly the length of each coat and the breadth between the shoulders. The men were then paired off with a coat that fit as *"near as possible according to his size"*.[127]

Thimbles and brass pins
c. 1758-1766
*Courtesy Fort Ligonier,
Ligonier, Pennsylvania*

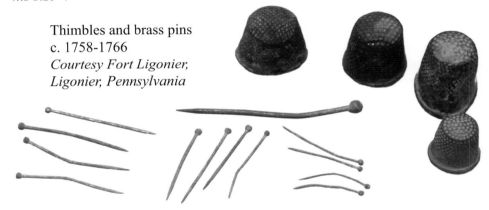

The length was altered so the coat tails ended just above the knee. The sleeves were lengthened or shortened so as to end at the joint of the wrists, and the cuffs were made just large enough for the hands to fit through, which according to Cuthbertson, provided more warmth and allowed for better mobility.[128] If the sleeves were too tight under the armpits, the seams were undone and gores were added.[129] If needed, the entire uniform was taken apart, altered, and reconstructed.

Tailor's thimble
c. 1750-1780
shown actual size
*Collection of the
Fort Ticonderoga Museum*

The order book of the 12th Regiment for May 12th, 1761 reads:

"In regards to the coats, the waist must be kept of a proper length, neither too short nor too long, the coat collar must come high so as to cover the stock buckle, lay smooth and not bind in wrinkles; the part of the coat it is sewed on must be full on the chest and high, the skirts of a proper length and hand so as to show the buckle on the knee-band of the breeches. Care to be taken to fit the sleeves well under the armpits, so as not to raise the skirts when the arm is lifted up. All the seams must be new sewed and smoothed, the lace double sewed in every part, the lining well fixed, red hearts on the inside skirts with a double loop of new red cloth, and button on instead of hooks and eyes, to be secured as well as possible, the red shoulder-strap in a straight line along the top of the shoulder".[130]

The breeches, as Cuthbertson suggested in 1768, should *"be made to fit smooth and tight upon the thighs, to cover well the knee-pan; to come very high upon the hips, with a broad waistband...".*[131] An order in the 12th Regiment in 1761 read:

"In fitting the breeches the tailors are to observe that they must fully cover the kneepan and be rather wide than tight along the thighs, and keep the waistband as high as possibly with a fork well opened".[132]

The waistcoat was fitted tight across the chest, made to come up as far as the lower button on the shirt neck, and end half way down the thigh.

"The Quartermaster to deliver to each Company two of the coats brought by Sergeant Lowry, these to be made into waistcoats, observing that they come up close to the lower button of the shirt neck, that the waist be full long, and the button of the pocket reaches within four inches of the upper button on the sides of the breeches".[133]

Any material left over from the uniform alterations was used to make fatigue caps, gloves, or other items for the men.[134] Cuthbertson recommended that a soldier's name be sewn or painted inside each article of his clothing to identify the owner. He also suggested that the name of the tailor who altered it be included. This ensured that if the workmanship was poor the offending tailor could be identified.[135] After the new uniforms were fitted the old clothing was cleaned and mended, or altered into new articles of clothing. The previous year's coat was either retained intact as a fatigue coat, or had the lace removed and cut down into a frock coat. Frequently old coats were taken apart and turned into a waistcoat, like those of the 12th Regiment in 1761:

"...we are all throng in riping our Old Coats to make our Waistcoats & Cleaning our lace".[136]

The coat skirts could be turned into a new pair of breeches, while the sleeves were sometimes sewn onto the old waistcoats, or made into gloves or caps. An old wool waistcoat could be restored by sewing on a new front or back piece. Old flannel waistcoats could be turned into a new pair of stockings, or shorter socks, as in the case of the 42nd Regiment in the fall of 1761:

"Each man to have also a pair of good socks which may be made out of old hose or old flannel waistcoats".[137]

After the soldier's new uniforms were fitted, they were reviewed by a general officer to see that they fit properly and were well sewn; those that were not were sent back to the tailor to be fixed:

"And this day all the Serjeants & Corporals was got Altered, and we put them on & was review'd by the Major to see how they fitted. And some was right & Others was not & Obliged to be return'd back to Taylors".[138]

The soldier's clothing and accouterments were examined weekly by the company officers. Any broken or lost buckles, straps, buttons, or other items were immediately replaced, and deducted from the offender's pay. This means a quantity of replacements were probably carried by each regiment. On no account was a soldier to swap uniforms or accouterments with another without the consent of an officer, nor was any soldier or officer to wear anything other than their regimental uniforms:

"Without his officer's consent, no soldier must presume to purchase from, or change his linen or necessaries with another soldier".[139]

New recruits entering a regiment were given surplus coats or simple wool jackets from the regimental stores until the next years clothing was issued.[140]

Opposite
Grenadiers, 13th, 14th and 15th
Regiments of Foot, 1751
by David Morier
The Royal Collection © 2007
Her Majesty Queen Elizabeth II

13
REGIMENT

14
REGIMENT

15
REGIMENT

Personal Care and Hygiene

One of the first things soldiers learned after enlisting was how to clean and care for themselves, their uniform and equipment, and how to dress, as Humphrey Bland described, in a *"soldier-like way"*.[141] One officer in 1762 wrote:

"There is a Kind of Science in dressing a Soldier, in teaching him to carry his Arms gracefully, to make him hold up his Head, and stand firm on his feet, and to make him wear his Cloaths and Hat genteely".[142]

Several articles were issued to each soldier for cleaning their clothing and maintaining their hygiene, including a stiff bristled coat brush, two shoe brushes, clay coloring balls, and two combs. Soap and other items had to be purchased privately.

Comb fragments
c. 1750-1780
shown actual size
*Collection of the
Fort Ticonderoga Museum*

The soldier's clothing was cleaned as often as needed, which according to Major Hawks the officers were to see done:

"It is further expected that the officers…see the men waish their shirts & stockens as often as needful…".[143]

It was not uncommon for the men to sleep without their shirts to save the expense of having to wash or replace them when dirty or worn out. This practice was recorded by a soldier of the 68th Regiment:

"…it was usual for the soldiers to lay without their shirts, both in camp and in quarters; as in the former the straw wears them out very fast, and in the latter it is done to avoid catching any distemper, as well as to save both the wash and wear, as a soldier can very ill afford to replace a shirt when worn out…".[144]

On other occasions, men went many days without removing their clothing and accouterments. Corporal Todd recorded the following after taking part in a raid on the coast of Normandy in 1758:

"I went & laid down in my hammock; not having my cloaths of[f] for those 10 days passt".[145]

A prescribed number of women were allowed to follow the army and were paid by the soldiers to wash, press, and mend their clothing. Wet clothing was never to be dried on the tents, as it was probably considered unsightly in a military camp, though it seems to have been a regular occurrence. Captain Stewart wrote in July of 1760:

"The men are to dry their shirts and hose near to the flank and rear of the battalion and not on their tents".[146]

Shoes constantly wore out as George Washington remarked when writing to Lord Loudoun in March of 1757:

"I have known a soldier go upon command with a new pair of shoes, which shoes perhaps have stood from seven shillings and sixpence to ten shillings, and return back without any; so much do they wear in wading creeks, fording rivers, clambering mountains covered with rocks, &c.".[147]

Any soldier previously employed as a shoe maker or cobbler before enlisting was put to work repairing shoes. Leather and tools for mending shoes were often readily available. In June of 1758, Colonel Bouquet wrote:

"The dew, and the roads full of sharp stones, will very soon wear out the 3 pairs of shoes that each soldier is to have, Besides the Leather which the campfollowers and merchants with the army will carry, with shoemaker's tools and wax to sew them".[148]

Corporal Todd wrote in his journal in December of 1761:

"George Dales, our Shoemaker, brought home my Shoes he had Soled…& gave him my Others to Sole".[149]

A return of Captain Blackwood's Pennsylvania company in May of 1758 listed 10 of the 53 soldiers as having been previously employed as shoe makers.[150]

Soldiers were to be clean shaven whenever they appeared under arms. Massachusetts Provincial Captain Jonathan Eddy recorded the following order in June of 1759:

"Whenever they turn out Under Arms On any Occasion whatsoever that they appear personally Neat and Clean, their beards shavd".[151]

Company barbers shaved the men and cut and dressed their hair. The barbers were soldiers formerly employed as barbers, or simply soldiers with some experience. Men took great pride in their hair, as Anne Grant, the daughter of an infantry officer recorded:

"Hair well dressed and in great quantity was then considered as the greatest possible ornament, which those who had it took the utmost care to display to advantage".[152]

The hair of the officers and private men was worn plaited, that is, braided and tied up under the hat with ribbon, or held in place with a small comb. Officers and highlanders sometimes wore their hair in a queue, which is a ribbon wrapped pigtail that hung down the back. The orderly book of the 12th Regiment for May 1st, 1761 reads:

"Cue ribbon to be provided immediately, and the Officers are desired to see that the men's hair are cut and dressed according to former orders".[153]

Private soldiers had a single side curl above their ears, while officers could have up to three. This ornamentation may have only been for parade, and not for field days. The soldier's hair was regularly combed in the morning and evening, as frequent combing was believed to promote hair growth. For this, each soldier was issued one or more combs made of bone, horn, or wood. The men's hair was oiled to keep it looking smooth, as Colonel Bagshawe stated:

"We begin to get their Hair in tolerable order, wch. I see every morning, that it be well comb'd, tyed, & oil'd to make it look smooth & well, & before next Review, it will all be long enou[gh] to plat & turn up under their Hats...".[154]

As this quote suggests, the men's hair was left to grow until it was long enough to plait. Cuthbertson recommended that the men's plaited hair should be untied and combed before they bedded for the night to help preserve it.[155]

Hair curler, c. 1750-1780
Collection of the
Fort Ticonderoga Museum

For Sunday parade and special reviews, the men's hair was powdered with white powder. A regimental order for the 42nd Foot on September 20th, 1761 stated:

"the men to curl their hair and put some powder in it in the evening before they go to bed, which will make it dress more easily in the morning, when it is again to be powdered and qued taking care to week the powder off their ears and necks".[156]

Any soldier who neglected his hair by letting it become tangled, dirty, or overrun with vermin, was liable to be punished. Soldiers who could not grow their hair long due to age or infirmity were *"obliged to provide themselves with wigs made to turn up like hair".*[157] Bland suggested that before any body of troops marched into a town, they halt briefly to *"give the men time to roll their cravats, cock their hats, and put themselves in the best order they can, that they may appear in a decent and soldier like manner upon entering the town".*[158]

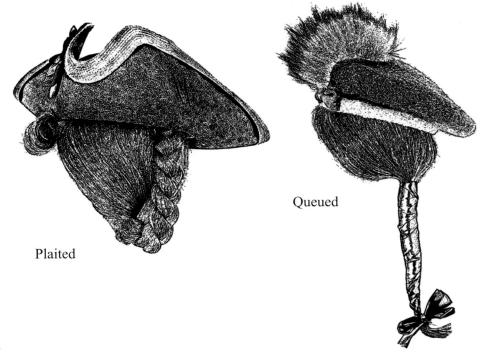

Plaited

Queued

52

"A South West View of the Lines at Fort Tyconderoga", 1759 - 1760. Thomas Davies
Library and Archives Canada, Acc. No. 1991-34-1

Camp Life and Diet

When a regiment was on the march, the quartermaster and camp colour men marched ahead to scout out a suitable location to camp for the night.[159] When one was found, they measured the company streets and marked them with sticks:

"When we came to our ground, as the old soldiers stiled it, we found several boughs stuck in the earth, as a mark where to fix our tents".[160]

As soon as they arrived in camp, the soldiers were directly employed in clearing and leveling the camp ground and erected their tents along the designated markers. Trees standing within the boundaries of the camp were cut down, the reasons for which Captain Stewart explains while encamped at Fort Ontario in 1760:

"The Regiments must not leave any tree standing within their encampments or so near to it or to the Qr Guards that if the winds should blow them down they can hurt any of the men".[161]

According to one soldier, with every hand employed, an encampment for a thousand men could be set up in less than half an hour:

"Every one was presently employed in setting up their little houses, and in less than half an hour the whole encampment, containing lodging for a thousand men, was completed".[162]

One of the first duties in a new camp was to set up "piquets" (guards posted around the perimeter of the camp) to prevent surprise attacks, and post guards throughout the camp to prevent fighting, looting, and drunkenness. The latrines were then dug, kitchens built, and foraging parties sent out to cut firewood and gather straw for the tents.

A private of the 68th regiment left us this detailed description of a military camp in 1758:

"The eight companies form eight separate streets, and each side of the street generally consists of ten tents, whos doors face the others opposite. At the front stand the Serjeant's tents, their doors do not face the street of the company, but look towards the front of the camp.

There is a Serjeant's tent at the end of every ten, and in front of his door is the bell tent, (two to each company) in which are kept all the men's firelocks. The Grenadiers form two half streets on the flanks of the other eight companies, and in the center of the front are the drums and colours of the regiment all in cases. About a hundred and fifty paces in front is the quarter guard of the regiment, which consists of an officer's marquee and six or eight tents for the men or guard to lay in. In the front of the guard is a bell-tent for the arms of the guard. In the rear of the men's tents is the subalterns line of marquees, then the Captains, and lastly the field officers; in the rear of all these is the chief sutler of the regiment, where the officers generally eat and drink, and in the rear of him are the petty sutlers, and likewise the bat-mens tents, who take care of the officer's horses and forage; and the cooking places, there is one of those to each company, which is a place cut in the ground, and earth thrown up to a heap , and the trench is the place where the kettles are fixed. In the rear of all are the places for easing nature, which consists of a long hole cut in the ground, with a pole fixed upon two forked ones, which the men sit. At night there is a guard that goes from the quarter guard and to the rear, which is called the rear guard, and which is to see that no disturbances happen in the sutlers tents & c. At the flanks of each regiment the camp-colours are fixed, which are generally of the same colour with the facings of the regiment".[163]

A "mess" of four to six soldiers slept together in one tent:

"The usual manner of laying is head to feet, three one way, and three the other...and it is a settled rule that the oldest soldier lies at the furthest end of the tent, and the youngest next to the door; which is not a very desirable situation, as every one who goes out or comes in is likely to tread on you".[164]

Spade with broad arrow stamp
c. 1760-1780
*Collection of the
Fort Ticonderoga Museum*

It was a good practice to keep the same tent mates together for as long as possible as they soon became acquainted with each other and their routines, but as vacancies opened due to death, desertions, and discharges, men were inevitably shuffled around. Private Luke Gridley of Connecticut wrote in his Diary in 1757:

"our tent mates had their tents took from us & we put into other tents".[165]

The British infantry tent was made of heavy, tightly woven hemp linen, measuring around eight feet long, six feet wide, and six feet tall, with a bell back for storing the men's hats and accouterments. The tents were erected with two upright poles and a ridge pole made of wood. It is possible that the tent poles were branded with the regiment, company, or mess numbers. A ledger for the 60th Regiment in 1759 included one pound for *"a set of brands to mark tent poles &c"*.[166]

The base of the tent was secured with sixteen hardwood tent pegs. The tent's door flaps did not tie shut, but were simply pinned at the base with a tent peg. The tents were pitched in straight lines, and any tent that was pitched irregularly had to be struck and re-pitched.[167] To prevent the tents of one company from intermixing with those of other companies or regiments, and to ensure that each mess lodged in their respective tents, each tent was painted with the number of the regiment, company, and mess.[168] It is possible that the tents came with cloth bags to store and carry them in, which is suggested in this letter written by Captain Schlosser to Colonel Bouquet in 1760:

"...I have lost the tents and as I have learned that the Pennsylvanians have brought to Presque Isle 2 tent bags, two tents, a uniform, and a blanket, I beg you to send them back to me".[169]

When old or damaged, tents could be mended by the regimental tailors, or turned into articles of clothing, as mentioned in the orderly book of Captain Stewart:

"The Tailors as they have finished the other work are immediately to repair the mens tents, the charge of which will be charged to the camp necessarys".[170]

"...the mens old tents to be cut down, washed and made into short drawers".[171]

Each tent was issued six bundles of straw for bedding (each bundle weighing roughly twenty pounds), with two new bundles of straw being issued every seven days.[172] When new straw was issued, the old straw was often burned. Colonel Bouquet recorded in his orderly book in June of 1758:

"The Camp Colour Men are to attend the Commissary for the distribution of provisions to their regiments; they are to assist in making the camp and keeping the streets and parade clean. To burn old straw when new is distributed, and throw fresh earth onto the Necessaries every two days".[173]

When straw was unavailable, it was substituted with sweet grass, spruce boroughs, or leaves:

"As fresh straw cannot be conveniently got for ye troops, it is recommended to ye officers to direct ye cutting of spruce bows".[174]

"A man of a tent to go for leaves for bedding".[175]

Wooden tent pegs
c. 1758-1766
*Courtesy Fort Ligonier,
Ligonier, Pennsylvania*

To prevent water from leaking under the tent, gutters were dug around the base to lead it away:

"To remedy this disaster of water penetrating the tents and wetting the straw...so many men of a tent were ordered to turn out and level the streets, and to cut gutters around the tents to carry the water off & c".[176]

When tents were unavailable, soldiers built brush huts, or simply slept in the open. Writing to John St. Clair in June of 1758, Colonel Bouquet wrote:

"...I have not yet received one Tent for these Troops and they must make shiffts for a few days with Bark, and build little hutts".[177]

To keep warm when sleeping in the open, large fires were built, which the men slept around with their feet towards the flames.[178] Each mess was issued two blankets for bedding, which were sometimes sewn together at the ends to *"prevent one man's having a greater share then another".*[179]

In America, where the weather was more severe, and straw was not as readily available, every soldier was issued his own blanket. The blankets were woven from white wool, sometimes with a dark stripe at each end, and stamped in the middle of one or both ends with a black "GR" and broad arrow. Blankets were carried in wagons or on horseback near the regiment. Army physician Donald Munro recalled in his book, published in 1764:

"Blankets ought to be provided for each Tent, and those carried along with the Regiment as to be always ready for the Men when they come to their Ground. During the late War in Germany, a Couple of Blankets were allowed for each Tent of the British Troops, and each Company carried their Blankets covered with an Oil Cloth on a Horse; so that they were always up with the Regiment when they came to their Ground".[180]

On occasions when soldiers needed to carry their blankets on their person, they could be tied to the knapsack, or possibly stuffed in it, worn tied around the body bandolier style, or worn over the shoulder with an improvised leather or rope shoulder strap. Besides the tent, poles, and bedding, each mess was issued a wooden mallet for driving tent pegs, a small axe for cutting wood, a tin cooking kettle with bag, and occasionally a bill hook, shovel, or spade:

"Every tent, or six men, have a hatchet, and a mallet for driving the tent pins into the ground, two standard poles, a ridge pole, and a large kettle...".[181]

Camp equipment was usually carried in wagons. When no wagons were available, a mess' camp equipment was divided up and carried by the men.

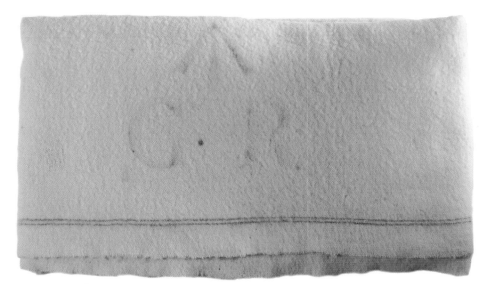

Military issue blanket, c. 1770-1777
Though this blanket dates from the time of the American Revolution, it is similar to those used from 1755-1768
Length: 68", Width: 90"
Collection of the
Fort Ticonderoga Museum

Wooden mallet head
c. 1758-1766
Courtesy Fort Ligonier,
Ligonier, Pennsylvania

The army's rations, or "King's Rations", were regulated by Parliament via the Treasury Board and the Commissary General's Office. The Commissary General determined what foodstuffs the infantryman would be issued, and in what quantities.[182] Flour, peas, cattle, hogs, and other provisions, were contracted for by the Commissary General's Office from victuallers (food suppliers) throughout Britain, and were inspected and sampled by the "Commissary of Stores".[183] The Commissary General employed butchers and laborers who prepared the provisions, and coopers and carpenters who constructed containers to transport them.[184] Provisions were delivered to the regimental agents, who in turn issued them to the regiment's quartermaster for inspection and distribution to the soldiers.[185]

Throughout the 1750s, a soldier's ration for the course of one week consisted of 7 pounds of bread or flour, 7 pounds of beef or 3 ½ pounds of pork, ½ pint of rice, 6 pints of peas, and 6 ounces of butter. If peas or rice were unavailable, an equivalent of meat, bread, oatmeal, corn, beans, or other provisions were given in their place. Loaves of bread called "ammunition bread" were baked in large quantities in ovens, which could be found at most outposts, or built within encampments for temporary use:

"We put an equal share of ammunition bread into the kettle, which bread is delivered to us on set days, and stopped out of our pay, it is as black as our hats, in general, and quite sour".[186]

Ammunition bread was baked in five to nine pound loaves. As the following examples demonstrate, the bakers needed to take into account the fact that the weight of flour did not equal the same weight in baked bread:

"No baker of this army will be allowed to take more than one penny sterling for baking 7 pounds of flour which makes a loaf of 9 pounds weight. Any of the Corps may get it baked cheaper if they can. It is recommended to the Commanding Officers of the Provincial Regimts to pay for the baking of their bread in the same manner, which the Regulars do, but if they pay in kind they are not to take 7 pounds of bread for 7 pounds of flour which is a shameful deduction from the portion allowd a soldier and too exorbitant a profit for the baker".[187]

Opposite
16th and 17th Regiments of Foot, and Grenadier and Drummer,
18th Royal Irish Regiment of Foot, 1751
by David Morier
*The Royal Collection © 2007
Her Majesty Queen Elizabeth II*

"...as seven Pounds of flour make Nine Pounds of Bread where you can not get Bread baked that quantity of flour is to be issued in lieu of the 9#. Bread".[188]

"The bakers must deliver at the rate of 120 lbs. weight of bread for 100 lbs. weight of flour".[189]

On the occasions when soldiers were issued raw flour, and ovens were unavailable, the flour was mixed with water and baked into "flour cakes" on hot ashes.[190] Large armies typically traveled with herds of cattle, hogs, or sheep, ready to be slaughtered to provide fresh meat for the soldiers. An entry in Colonel Bouquet's orderly book in 1764 reads:

"The oxen and sheep will move behind the baggage in separate droves and properly guarded, The provisions will follow the cattle in four divisions, each conducted by a Horse master, and consisting of four brigades of pack horses".[191]

Every piece of meat was utilized, and little was wasted. *"A Bullock's head is to be issued for eight pounds of beef, a tongue for three pound, a heart for its weight",*[192] wrote Captain Knox in July of 1759:

However, the necks, hoofs, and legs, were not widely used by the regular army. In American, these unused portions were given to the provincials, as Colonel John Armstrong informed Governor Denny of Pennsylvania:

"...the Victuallers, notwithstanding the Cheapness and Poorness of the Beef, salt up and deliver to the Soldiers all the Necks, Houghs & Shins which I am informed are never given to the Regular Troops in his Majesties Service, who are generally supplyed with the best Beef...".[193]

Whenever fresh meat and bread were unavailable, which was common on campaign or foreign service, the equivalent of salted meat and biscuit were issued. "Biscuits" were small wheels of bread made of flour and water baked rock hard. It was common when issuing several days rations to issue it partly in fresh and partly in salted provisions. Besides victuals, rum was also issued to the soldiers. The allowance of rum recorded by Knox as being issued to the men of the 43rd Regiment in August of 1759 was the common allowance throughout the army:

"As the Government has provided good store of Rum for the men, half a jill may be delivered out regularly every day, and a jill when the weather is wet and cold, or when the men are much fatigued with work or duty".[194]

Rum rations were usually ordered to be diluted with water at the rate of two to eight gills of water to one gill of rum. In his orderly book for May 21st, 1755, Colonel Sir Peter Hawkett of the 44th Regiment wrote:

"One Jill of Rum mixt with Three Jills of Water may be Allowd to Each man per Day, which the officers of the picquet are to see delivered out every day at 11 o'Clock...".[195]

On no account was any soldier to give or sell his rum ration to another:

"Whenever Rum is to be issued out to the troops...any soldier who is known to have disposed of his allowance to another, or any one who will make any agreement on receiving such allowance...shall be entirely out of ye roll when Rum is delivered out, besides ye punishment".[196]

In America, spruce beer was commonly brewed; not only was it good for the health of the men by helping to prevent scurvy, but the officers also profited from its sale:

"The allowance per man was two quarts per day to each man, or three and one half gallons per week, for which he paid seven pence...The paymaster for the 43rd regiment assures me, that the spruce account for that corps in the space of about 7 weeks, amounted to eighty pounds currency".[197]

Captain Knox recorded the recipe for making spruce beer in 1757:

"It is made from the tops and branches of the spruss-tree, boiled for 3 hours, then strained into casks, with a certain quantity of melasses, and as soon as cold it is fit for use".[198]

Up to two quarts of spruce beer was allowed each soldier every day:

"when we were incamped at Halifax the allowance (of spruce beer) *was two quarts per day to each man, or 3 gallons and a half per week"*.[199]

Soldier's sometimes made punch by mixing their spirits with water, sugar, molasses, lemon juice, vinegar, and spices.[200]

The King's Ration could be supplemented at the soldier's own expense from regimental sutlers who sold a variety of goods including fresh fruit, vegetables, eggs, poultry, cheese, milk, tea, and liquor.[201] Soldiers could sometimes buy food at the markets of nearby towns. Occasionally, citizens were allowed to set up markets near army camps.[202] Vegetables such as cabbage, potatoes, and beets were grown in the gardens supplying some outposts. Fruits were sometimes plucked from orchards when conveniently nearby, and salads were made from the leaves of dandelions.[203]

Food often had to be carried by the men, for which occasions haversacks were issued. The square haversack was made of linen, with a button down flap, and a shoulder strap made of matching linen, as seen below, or leather, as seen in Morier's painting of the 49th Regiment Grenadier shown on page 124. The haversack was marked on the back with a 'GR' and broad arrow, and sometimes with the soldier's regiment or company number.[204] A ledger from the 60th Regiment in 1759 included £17 13s 4d spent on *"marking and numbering 1060 haversacks, and a like number of knapsacks"*.[205]

The haversack was worn high up under the right arm above the cartridge pouch. It is possible that the regimental tailors adjusted the cloth shoulder straps to the proper length for each soldier, as the same ledger from the 60th Regiment also included funds spent on *"altering 730 haversacks"*.[206]

When needed, food could be carried in the knapsack or coat pockets:

"When the troops are ordered to land, the first body at Gabarus Bay must carry nothing in the boats but their arms and ammunitions with bread and cheese in their pockets for two days".[207]

Every soldier was issued a canteen made of tin plated iron which held up to a quart of water or spirits:

"...and every man hath a canteen of tin to carry water or any other liquor, which will hold upwards of a Quart".[208]

The canteen was worn on a hemp cord over the right shoulder, hanging on the left side, which kept the water filled canteen away from the gun powder filled cartridge pouch, and the food filled haversack. Two styles of canteens were used by the army, the body of one being kidney shaped, and the other crescent shaped. To plug the opening, a wooden stopper or formed tin cap was used.[209]

Linen haversack, with 'GR' and broad arrow, c. 1750-1780
This haversack, having been folded in half, has left a backwards imprint of the 'GR' and broad arrow. The original is now corroded.
Length: 13.5", Width: 16.75"
Courtesy Col. J. Craig Nannos

Crescent shaped tin canteen
c. 1750-1780
Length: 8.89", Width: 5.32"
Courtesy Col. J. Craig Nannos

Each mess was issued one large tin kettle for cooking their rations. The kettles held between eight and ten quarts, and came with a tin lid and cloth carrying bag. Copper kettles were sometimes issued,[210] and occasionally cast iron kettles, as depicted in the Morier paintings shown on pages 63 and 69. The kettles may have been marked with the number of the regiment, company, or mess, as a ledger from the 60th Regiment in 1759 included seven shillings for *"marking and mending camp kettles"*.[211] A list of stores sent to America in 1754 for the artillery, civil officers, and artificers, included forty camp kettles with frying pan covers.[212]

Right
Remnants of a tin mess kettle
c. 1758-1766
Courtesy Fort Ligonier,
Ligonier, Pennsylvania

Each soldier took a turn to receive and cook the rations for his fellow messmates, and was cleared from duty for that day:

"The Serjeants are to warn the Men for Duty by Tents or Messes so as one Man at least of a Mess may be left in Camp to Cook for the Rest".[213]

"The officer of the Guard to see that there is one man Cleared from duty Every day from Each Mess to Cook each one for his Mess and that there no one presume to boil their meet before it is well freshened and Cleaned and that ye Pease be boild Soft before the meat be put In...".[214]

Kidney shaped tin canteen,
with hemp strap and tin cap
c. 1750-1780
Length: 8.71", Width: 6.75"
Courtesy Col. J. Craig Nannos

Those soldiers who were on guard duty were not allowed to leave their post to eat, so their food was brought to them by a member of their mess.[215]

Meat was never to be broiled, but boiled with peas, rice, and other provisions into soup, as Major Hawks ordered in 1759:

"It is further expected that the officers see the men cook their victuals properly and not to broil pork on any account whatsoever".[216]

"Commanding officers of Companys are to see that their men boil their fresh meat & make soop as it will be much more for their heath & go further".[217]

It was strongly recommended that the soldiers not eat their salt provisions until they were properly "freshened", as Knox explained:

"As it is impossible to get fresh provisions for the troops in our present situation, for the preservation of the soldiers' health it is absolutely necessary to give the utmost attention to freshening and boiling pork, which ought to be done in the following manner: Pork or beef to be steeped at least twenty hours, changing the water three times, scraping and washing the salt off each time that the water is removed, and then boil it with peas as usual".[218]

Cooking was done on open fires at the rear of the camp, away from the tents. When encamped for an extended period, company size "camp kitchens" were built. A camp kitchen was made by digging a round trench, piling the dirt into a mound in the center, and cutting holes into the sod at its base, which acted as an earthen stove for cooking. Bland's 1759 treatise gives us the following dimensions of a camp kitchen:

"The inner diameter of the kitchens is sixteen feet, surrounded by a trench three feet broad...".[219]

.This method of cooking conserved heat, used less firewood, and the small holes protected the fire from rain. Each mess was issued twenty pounds of dry wood a day for cooking and warmth, or forty pounds of green wood.[220] The Pioneers under Corporal Todd in 1761 cut their firewood into lengths of *"about half a yard".*[221] Eating and cooking utensils like knives, spoons, forks, and bowls, were non-issue items, and had to be purchased or made individually; some soldiers simply went without. Regarding eating utensils, a soldier of the 68th Foot remarked: *"some had knives, while others had none; as to spoons and forks, we were all in one case, destitute, and no porringers or bowls".*[222] However, it would appear from the amount of surviving examples that knives and spoons were regularly used; they were even included in a list of equipment carried by a grenadier on the march compiled by Lieutenant Baillie in 1762, which can be seen on page 78. A list calculating the provisions and stores necessary for four hundred men in 1756 included fifty wooden bowls and five hundred spoons.[223]

Food was not always plentiful. Supply lines could be stretched thin or cut off by the enemy, sufficient numbers of wagons, draft animals and boats used for the transportation of goods were often hard to acquire, and meat and flour easily spoiled, or were outright bad to begin with. In 1758, Captain Knox described the beef his soldiers were supplied with as *"...much inferior to some I have frequently seen condemned and burned publicly in well-regulated towns in Europe".*[224] Condemned food was sometimes sold, as Lord Loudoun ordered when in Halifax in July of 1757:

"All provisions furnished by the contractors that has been surveyed and condem'd to be sold by the commesarry of provisions for the benefit of the Crown".[225]

Other times, condemned food was fed to the horses, as Captain Stewart recorded in October of 1759:

"The damaged provisions surveyed this day and condemned is ordered to be thrown in to the Lake except the bread which is ordered to be kept for the horses".[226]

More often, condemned food was buried, burned, or in some other way discarded. It was not unheard of for contractors to short change or cheat their customers. In a letter to Colonel Bouquet, one army captain wrote:

"I wish the barrels were opened & inspected before they were put in board, for there is great cheating somewhere. There Are often deficiencies...A barril opened 2 days Ago was one half of it filled up with stones & Sticks. Two barrils of pork were quite full of pork, but so rotten that there was no coming near it".[227]

In a letter to Governor Denny of Pennsylvania in 1756, Colonel Armstrong complained:

"...the Beef bought in these parts is generally ill fed, and the most of it is not above two or three years old".[228]

When food was scarce, rations had to be reduced, or money issued in their place, typically at the rate of four pence per ration.[229] In desperation, starving soldiers turned to eating animals such as dogs, cats, and mice.[230]

19
REGIMENT

20
REGIMENT

Ro. N. BRIT
FUZILEERS

It was not unknown for a quartermaster or officer to reject the provisions or cattle acquired for them. In a letter to George Washington in 1758, General Forbes wrote:

"...I am told Mr. Rutherford's complaint is occasioned by Col. Bouquet is having refused some cattle of Mr. Walker's that really was not fit to be used in our way".[231]

At other times, food was so plentiful that soldiers could draw as much as they pleased, such as in General Braddock's army at the onset of his 1755 campaign:

"As an Encoredgement to the men & to promote their Diligence And Activity Every man will be allowd every day as much fresh or salt provision & bread or Flower, without any stoppag for the same, As long & in as great proportions as it will be posable to provide them unless any man should be found drunk, Negligent or Disobedient, in such case this gratuity shall be stopped".[232]

While in France in 1758, Corporal Todd made the following entry in his journal on August 10th:

"The provest guard brought a great many more cattle into camp about 11 O clock, & the general order is that all the butchers in the army assemble in the rear & kill & dress the best of the cows and beasts etc [&] hang them up in the trees, that the men may take & cook what they please".[233]

Bullocks and hogs were slaughtered throughout the year and salted for the use of the campaigning army, and for use during the winter. Slaughtering was preferably done in the cooler months, as the summer heat easily spoiled meat during the preserving process. When encamped for an extended period of time, tents were erected for storing the provisions, fences were made to enclose the cattle,[234] wells were dug to making fetching water more convenient,[235] and ovens were built for baking bread. When the weather turned cold, huts of wood or brush were built for the men to live in, or large wooden frames interwoven with branches called "hurdles" were place over the tents and covered with sod for added protection and insulation.

Opposite
Grenadiers, 19th and 20th Regiments of Foot,
and 21st Royal North British Fusiliers, 1751
by David Morier
The Royal Collection © 2007
Her Majesty Queen Elizabeth II

Corporal Todd recorded the following while fighting in Germany in October of 1761:

"Lord Granby gave Orders for the Men to make Hutts to Cook & sit in the day time & to Hurdle their tents & thatch them over with anything they can find. So now everyone is Employ'd, some going for wood, whilst Others are diging the ground for the Hutts as the men in ever[y] tent makes one for themselves, & sods them over etc.".[236]

Cuthbertson describes the method and advantages of hurdling tents:

"the most expeditious and ready method, is, to provide square hurdles, large enough to cover a Tent, when resting slope ways against the upper edge of each other; they must be above a foot on every side longer than the Tent, to leave sufficient Room for striking: a piece of wicker-work is next to be fitted to the front, by way of a door, to move at pleasure: these hurdles and wickers being properly made and fixed, a thick coat of thatch (either straw, sedge, or rushes) is to be laid on them, well secured and bound: nothing can be warmer than one of these habitations, when the Soldiers are in it, have drawn to the door, and pinned the Tent quite close on every side: huts dug into the earth, or built with sods , are, at an advanced season of the year, extremely damp, and of course unhealthy, for the Soldiers; the hurdle ones, on the contrary, are always dry, as the front can be entirely laid open in fair weather, by removing the wicker door, and turning up the bottom of the Tent, in such a manner, that the air may have an interrupted passage round the inside of them".[237]

Soldiers were informed of any general orders in the mornings, usually at roll call:

"The Orderly Officer of each Company is to see that the Publick orders of each day be Read & Explain'd to the Soldiers of his Company".[238]

Soldiers were kept constantly busy, and were not to lie idle in their tents or huts, as idle soldiers were more likely to cause trouble. Wolfe, while stationed in Scotland, made sure that his new recruits and troublesome soldiers did not associate with other men of similar nature, and were instead quartered with good sober men:

"Loose disorderly fellows were not to be allowed to mess, lye, or any how associate together, and great care was to be taken to put recruits and young soldiers into messes with sober good men".[239]

"A South View of Crown Point, Lake Champlain", 1759. Thomas Davies
Library and Archives Canada, Acc. No. 1991-33-2

The majority of the soldier's time was spent drilling, marching, keeping their arms and accouterments clean, and performing various manual tasks. Besides this, every soldier took his turn performing guard duty:

"...they (the soldiers) must stand centinel, and be upon pickets and other outposts in the Night, during all Kinds of Weather; besides performing Duties; and when near an enemy, they are perhaps on duty every second or third night, besides working parties, and other duties of fatigue".[240]

Inspections were a common occurrence. The clothing, tents, arms, and accouterments were inspected once a week or more by an officer. Every day when the weather permitted the tents and blankets were aired out and cleaned:

"Leit. Col. Winslow orders that the tents of the two Battallions of Governor Sherlys Regiment be this Day thoroughly Cleansed the Blankets Aird and that in order to do it Let ye tents be Struck or at Least that the pins be Losened".[241]

The Articles of War were regularly read to the soldiers which explained to them the consequences of deserting, theft, mutiny, and other crimes:

"...and the General orders that the articles of War be immediately and frequently read, and that every body may be informed all neglects or disobedience of them or any Orders will not be forgiven".[242]

"The Articles of War to be read at 12 o'Clock to the Soldiers under Arms Viz^t Sect^n 2^d Mutiny, 6th Desertion, 13th Stores & Ammunition, 14th The Articles 4th, 5th, 6th, 9th, 10th, 11th, 12th, 13th, 14th, 15th, & 23rd, and the 1st Article of the 19th Section".[243]

The tents were struck and washed regularly, often in salt water to keep the canvas from rotting, as Captain Stewart noted in 1760, and again in 1761:

"The mens tents and bells of arms to be struck tomorrow morning at 5 o'clock, if fair, and washed to prevent them rotting".[244]

"The new tents to be pitched tomorrow morning, but are first to be dipped in salt water, to prevent their being mildewed".[245]

The soldiers belonging to a tent found by an officer to be dirty could be confined and punished, as this general order issued by Lord Loudoun in 1757 explains:

"...an off^r of a Company Visit ye Mens Tents in Order to Se that they Are Kept as Clean as Possible & if any of ye Tents are Found after this Day with any Filth or Durt in them the Visiting off^r is Emediately to Order S^d Tent to be Struct & Cleaned - & the Men Who He Judges to Be Guilty of this Neglect are Emmediately to Be Confined for Disobedience of Orders".[246]

The camp's streets were constantly swept clean. When muddy, the streets were covered with bark, straw, or tree branches:

"...Commanding off^r of the Diferent Corps se that ye Streets of their Respective Encampments Be Swept Clean Every Day...".[247]

"Whenever ye weather permit ye Commdg off^r of Each Corp are to order their mens tents to be Struck, ye Bark to be laid out in ye Street & ye Ground turn.d up".[248]

Occasionally, soldiers had to perform duties such as policing city streets, capturing wanted criminals,[249] guarding civil functions, and working as firemen. Soldier labor was used to construct forts, dig entrenchments, build and repair roads, make gardens, and load and unload cargo from ships. Some jobs paid an extraordinary wage, while others were considered a soldier's duty and never paid:

"When any of ye troops Regulars or Provincials during the campaign are employed as artificers or labourers they will be paid for the same at ye following rates in New York currency; all artificers pr diem 1/3; to mortar makers & labourers & workers of ye kind 1/-; Other labourers in work such as building storehouses or barracks or hospitals 19d. All other works such as intrenchments making Forts, or parties mending of roads, they are the soldiers duty and never paid".[250]

Soldiers worked six to eight hours or more a day with breaks for breakfast or dinner. Colonel Bouquet recorded the following regulations for the workers at Albany in 1756:

"The Artificers and Laborers are to Parade at 6 oclock...and are to work 9 hours every day, from six to twelve; half an hour being allowed for Breakfast, and in the afternoon from half an hour after two, till six at Night, for which each laborer is to be Paid, nine Pence pr day, and every Artificer employ'd as above fifteen pence, and every Serjeant fifteen pence, pr day, all New York currency".[251]

In their off time, soldiers could earn extraordinary wages by working in nearby towns or farms as laborers; this was very common during the harvesting season:

"The soldiers that have leave to reap are to make up the duty they have missed to their companies".[252]

If a soldier had any previous professions, as many did, they were sometimes allowed to work at their trade outside the regiment, but were never to be seen wearing any article distinguishing their trade with their uniform:

"...nor is any man to be seen in the streets with a leathern apron or other mark of his profession and his Regimental coat on".[253]

Wolfe issued the following orders specifying who was allowed to work outside of his regiment, and who was not:

"It is order'd that upon no account whatever any future indulgence be given to such of the working men as have misbehaved, contracted debts, or appear'd dirty and slovenly, and they are strictly forbid hereafter to work under severe penalty. The soldiers that have leave to reap are to make up the duty they have missed to their companies...only sober and healthy men wer to be detailed for such duty. No recruits were to be sent, and auckward men were not to go unless they happened to be paviors, carpenters, smiths, miners, and bricklayers".[254]

"No man that has ever been convicted of theft is to be sent to work at Lord Glenorky's nor any that have been often try'd by Court Martial unless there is a visible reform, least their behavior bring reproach upon the regiment".[255]

Jobs such as carrying coal, dirt, or filth, were not permitted, as they easily dirtied the men, their clothing, and according to Wolfe, was unbefitting a soldier, and brought dishonor to the Regiment.[256]

When doing jobs such as sweeping, carrying wood, water, straw, or performing other camp duties, the soldiers, if they had them, wore fatigue caps instead of their cocked hats. Fatigue caps were often made of scrap cloth left over from the regimental tailors, or made from the soldier's old clothing; other times they were contracted from tailors.[257]

Soldiers were paid using currency from a variety of countries, besides their own, such as Spain, Portugal, Mexico, Bolivia, France, and the American colonies. Europe traded on the gold and silver standard where the value of a coin was determined by the bullion it contained, not its country of origin. However, nations had different weight standards and denominations, and thus it was important for the paymaster or agent to receive and issue the diverse types of specie *"in an exact and equal proportion of value, one with another".*[578]

General Braddock wrote to the Duke of Newcastle, First Lord of the Treasury, in March of 1755:

"As small coined Silver will be greatly wanted for payment of the Troops, and as no considerable Quantity of it can be got in this Province; I must beg of your Grace to direct the Contractors, Mr. Hanbury & Mr Thomlinson, to send over as soon as possible, if they have not already done it, four or five Thousand pounds, in Piastrines & Half Piastrines: which is the more necessary, as all the Money already brought over by the Regimental Paymaster is in Spanish Gold and Dollars".[259]

No soldier could leave camp without permission from an officer, so entertainment had to be found within the confines of the camp.[260] Sutler's tents were popular places for soldiers to socialize and spend their money. The sutlers were located at the rear of the camp, between the kitchens and the rear guard. Here, soldiers could buy extra food, stationery, cloth, tobacco, pipes, snuff, and liquor.[261] Gambling occurred, though it was strictly forbidden, and those caught, as well as any onlookers, were liable to be punished:

"If any non-commissioned Officer or soldier shall be found gaming, he shall immediately receive three hundred lashes. And the standers by be deemed principals and punished as such".[262]

British coins
shown actual size
Courtesy John Neitz

sixpence
1757

halfpenny
1752

shilling
1743

Spanish 2 reales "pistareen"
shown actual size
The Colonial Williamsburg Foundation

pistareen
1721

Jaw harp
c. 1754
shown actual size
*Jumonville, Braddock Road
Preservation Association*

Music and singing could probably be heard often in camp. Some 18th century soldier's and sailor's songs are still being sung today. Occasionally, fighting broke out among soldiers, sometimes with lethal results, as Henry Foster observed in 1758:

"Two regulars went without the breastwork to fight and one killed the other the first pass that he made at him".[263]

Soldiers were permitted to go swimming in the mornings and evenings,[264] but were not to wade or swim in their regimental clothes.[265] Guards were placed over the designated swimming areas to prevent deserting.

Some soldiers were allowed to hunt game, but only with a signed pass, and not within a mile of the camp:

"No person to be Allowed to go hunt or kill game without a Pass Signed by ye Gen^lls A.D. Camp in which is to be Specifyd ye Number of ye Party & ye Reg^ts they belong too…".[266]

"No Person is to go a hunting without leave from Capt. Bartman Gen^ll Webb's A.D. Camp, & then not to fire within a mile of ye Camp".[267]

Occasionally, lotteries were held in which tickets were drawn to go hunting. The winners were allowed to eat or sell whatever they shot.[268]

Soldiers could apply to their commanding officers for furloughs, which were usually only allowed during the winter months after the campaign season ended. Only two men per company were allowed furloughs at a time.[269] Furloughs had to be applied for and signed by the company commander and were issued for a specific length of time, usually no more than one or two months. Every soldier going on furlough left his arms and accouterments in the company stores and had to pay for their upkeep.

If a soldier wished to marry, he first had to have the consent of his officer, as the following order issued by James Wolfe while stationed in Scotland states:

"Any soldier that presumes to marry clandestinely wanting credible winesses, and shall neglect the publick ceremonies of the Church, or shall not consult his Officer before his marriage that the woman's character may be enquir'd into – every such offender will be punish'd with vigour".[270]

However, it was preferable that officers discouraged their men from marrying, as Wolfe described in 1751:

"The Officers are desir'd to discourage Matrimony amongst the men as much as possible. The Service suffers by the multitude of Women already in the Regiment".[271]

"The Lieut-Colonel further Recommends to the Soldiers not to Marry at all; the long March and Embarkation that will soon follow must convince them that many Women in the Regiment are very inconvenient, especially as some of them are not so industrious nor so useful to their Husbands as a Soldier's Wife ought to be".[272]

A number of holidays and other special events were celebrated in the army including Christmas, Whitsunday, Saint Andrew's day, Saint George's day, the king's birthday, and the day of his accession to the throne:

"Christmas-day is at length come round…this grand festival was duly observed by the Chaplins of the garrison to a numerous congregation, as in England".[273]

"St. George's anniversary was duly observed by all the garrisons".[274]

"It being Whitsunday, this festival was duly observed".[275]

"The 1st Royal Highland Regiment to be under arms to morrow at 12 o'clock. They will fire 3 volleys in answer to three Royal Salutes from the Artillery, in honour of His Majesty's Birthday".[276]

 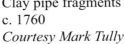

Clay pipe fragments
c. 1760
Courtesy Mark Tully

22
REGIMENT

Roᴸ Wᵗ
FUZILEERS

24
REGIMENT

Divine service was held every Sunday, usually at the head of each regiment. Sermons were given by regimental chaplains, or if unavailable, by an officer:

"Each Regiment is to have Divine Service performed at the head of their respective Colours every Sunday".[277]

There was no formal postal system in the British army, but mail was available for both officers and privates alike. The massive size of the British navy and their domination of the seas during the last half of the Seven Years War meant that letters could be mailed throughout the empire. Outgoing mail was given with postage to the regimental officer designated to receive it. The mail then made its way by courier to the nearest post office, and from there to the first naval or private ship heading to the appropriate destination:

"The General will send Dispatches to England this Day; any Officers that have Letters to send will give them in earlie to-morrow to Mr. Appie".[278]

Mail was also put aboard small cargo ships called "packets" which made regular trips on fixed routes:

"The Duke of Cumberland, packet boat, arrived from Falmouth, sailed the 15th of June and brought letters of the 12th from London".[279]

Because mail was delivered on foot, by horse, and by ship, it could take several days, weeks, or months before a letter was received, and because battalions were constantly on the move, letters were easily misplaced, as Knox complained in 1758:

"We are credibly informed that upwards of 40 letters for the officers and soldiers of the 43rd Regiment lately lay at the Post Office at Halifax, and the Postmaster, not knowing how he should be repaid the postage of them or were to forward them to, transmitted them back to New York. By which means it is not Improbable but they may all miscarry, it is an unlucky circumstance that some regulation is not set on foot, to prevent such disappointments happening to the troops".[280]

Knox continues to describe the postal system during the previous war, the War of the Austrian Succession (1740-1748):

"During the late war in Flanders, there was a Postmaster-General to the British Army, whose office was always at the headquarters, and all letters, whether forwarded by the packets to Holland, or transmitted by Private ships, or otherwise were regularly sent to the army and duly distributed to the respective regiments...".[281]

Official military correspondences were paid for by the crown, though this was not always possible. Captain John Schlosser writing to Colonel Bouquet from Philadelphia in 1764 stated:

"The post stages of the Letters wrote for sake of Duty have always been free, being payed by the king till I came here where I must pay for a single Letter 15, and for a Bigger one 30 pence Pensylv: currency...".[282]

Every night, at a time specified by general orders, the drummers beat "Tattoo", at which time every soldier was to be in his tent, and all fires and lights, except those of the guards, were to be extinguished:

"The Officers of the Quarter Guard to send a Corpl: & a file of men every Night at 9 oClock, And to see all lights Are Extinguished in the Soldiers Tents, And is frequently to send Patroles Round the Regts as fare as his Centrys Are posted, to see that every thing is quiet".[283]

Folding knife
c. 1750-1780
Shown actual size
Private collection

Opposite
Grenadiers, 22nd Regiment of Foot,
23rd Regiment, Royal Welch Fusiliers,
and 24th Regiment of Foot, 1751
by David Morier
*The Royal Collection © 2007
Her Majesty Queen Elizabeth II*

Overleaf
Grenadiers, 25th, 26th, and 27th Inniskilling Regiments of Foot,
and Grenadiers, 28th, 29th, and 30th Regiments of Foot, 1751
by David Morier
*The Royal Collection © 2007
Her Majesty Queen Elizabeth II*

25
REGIMENT

26
REGIMENT

INNISKILLING
REGIMENT

28
REGIMENT

29
REGIMENT

30
REGIMENT

Health

The men's physical health was an important factor in their performances as soldiers. General John Forbes realized the importance of making the soldier's lives comfortable *"without which no real service can be expected of them"*.[284] In his "Instructions for Young Officers", Wolfe recommended that they observe the appearance of the men under their command and send to the hospital any that looked ill:

"They are to attend the looks of the men, and if they are thinner or paler than usual the reasons may be enquired into, and proper means used to restore them".[285]

The men were ordered to bathe regularly, wash their hands and faces daily,[286] and change their wet shoes and stocking whenever possible. Diet was a key factor regarding the soldier's health, as General Wolfe observed in 1758:

"The army is undone and ruined by the constant use of salt meat and rum".[287]

The officers were to see that the men's food was properly cooked and that they did not eat their salt provisions without being properly prepared. Rum, wine, hard cider, and spruce beer were issued to help combat scurvy. Strict orders were given to the 20th Regiment in 1753 not to *"allow men to drink from standing pools, or any kind of dirty water, as the Surgeon is of opinion that it tends to give them the Bloody Flux"*.[288] To help combat the effects of bad water, soldiers were sometimes provided with ginger or vinegar to mix with the water in their canteens, as Anne Grant recorded in her memoirs:

"a quantity of powdered ginger was given to every man, and the Sergeants were ordered to see that when, in the course of marching, the soldiers arrived hot and tired at the banks of any stream, they should not be permitted to stoop and drink...but obliged to lift water into their canteens, and mix ginger with it. This became afterwards a general practice".[289]

Most fortresses had gardens where fresh vegetables could be had to help prevent scurvy:

"A Man of Each Mess of yᵉ 35ᵗʰ Regt. & of yᵉ Detachment of yᵉ 62ⁿᵈ Regᵗ Who are in Garrison at Fort-Edward To attend yᵉ Gardener at 10 oClock Tomorrow Morning Who will Deliver them out Vegetables to serve The Regᵗˢ".[290]

Fruits and vegetables could sometimes be purchased from the company sutler, or were sometimes taken from orchards, but were never to be eaten unless ripe. Constant exposure to the sun burned and tanned the skin, as there was no other protection than the soldier's clothing and hat. In March of 1743, Major Davenport wrote:

"I have slept three nights upon the ground, rolled up in my cloak without any covering except the sky, and my skin, or rather my hide – which is well tanned".[291]

Traveling hospitals containing surgeons, apothecaries, physicians, nurses, and commissaries followed large armies. The medical staff sent from England for General Braddock's 1755 campaign consisted of two master surgeons, two master apothecaries, six surgeon's and apothecary's mates, and one matron.[292]

Every regiment had its own surgeon, one or more surgeon's mates, and a medical chest containing surgical tools and medicines. Regimental surgeons were commissioned officers, and were *"obliged to pass an examination at Surgeons Hall before they are appointed"*.[293] Likewise, Donald Munro recommended that apothecaries *"ought in like manner to pass an examination at Apothecary hall"*,[294] and that *"No person ought to be appointed a Physician to the Army, or military hospital, without previously undergoing the same examination at the college of Physicians, as those who enter fellows and Licentiates of the college, that none but proper persons may be employed"*.[295] Munro's recommendations to the Physician General for protecting himself against infection included having *"a suit of cloaths reserved for visiting the hospital, and a waxed linen coat to wear above them in going round the wards"*.[296] Regimental physicians and surgeons may have worn similar garments.

Large tents were erected for hospitals and to house sick and wounded soldiers. When time and resources permitted, wooden huts were built. The hospitals were stocked with a variety of medicines, surgical instruments, bandages, clothing, food, alcohol, and bed sets.[297] In a letter to George Washington in 1756, Adam Stephen requested *"half a dozen of Bed-panns for the Hospital"*.[298] The hospital's tents, bedding, and equipment, traveled in wagons or on horseback. A quantity of bedding often traveled on horseback near to the army so as to be quickly accessed in an emergency. When in quarters or encamped near a town, hospitals were set up inside churches, warehouses, or other large enclosed structures, preferably on high ground.[299]

Ships were sometimes set up as floating hospitals, though inland hospitals were much preferred by the sick, as the mortality rate was much higher aboard hospital ships. Robert Kirk of the 42nd Regiment noted in his memoirs:

"I was sent with a number of sick, on board the hospital ship, for the recovery of my health, where for want of fresh air and room to stir, they almost all died".[300]

Cleanliness was a high priority. The hospitals were cleaned daily and regularly fumigated by sprinkling damp gunpowder or frankincense on hot coals.[301] Every sick man, as soon as he was received at the hospital, was first cleaned by washing or bathing in warm water, his clothing was removed and washed, and clean clothing issued in their stead.[302] In December of 1759, those soldiers of the 43rd Regiment sent to the general hospital were to receive *"two shirts, one cap, one jacket, two pair of stockings, and one good pair of shoes".*[303]

Every morning the patients were given warm water, soap, and a towel to clean their hands, feet, and faces. If they were too weak to wash themselves then they were washed by the nurses. The patients had their hair combed every day, and were shaved twice a week or more often if needed.[304] Even with these precautions, the hospitals were still quite unsanitary, and soldiers easily became riddled with flies and lice, as one sick soldier noted:

"...I came to myself so much to know that the Body Lice were eating me up, and told one of those who waited on me to heat a tailor's goose which was in the room, and ironed my blanket on both sides, which he did, and it turned it as red as blood".[305]

In order to keep track of the hospitalized soldiers and their equipment, each soldier was sent to the general hospital with *"...a Certificate, signed by an Officer of his Company, setting forth his name, Regiment, and Company, to what day he is subsisted, and what Arms and Accouterments he carries with him, which are to be bundled up and marked with the man's name, regiment, and company".*[306]

Surgeons also acted as dentists, extracting broken and infected teeth, which as Colonel George Mercer described, could be an extremely painful process:

"...I believe no man ever felt more cruel Torture than myself. A Gentleman of the physical Tribe prescribing drawing of a Tooth as the surest Cure for the Pain, broke the Tooth & at the same Stroke was so extremly lucky as to fracture my Jaw Bone which for twenty odd days made Me delirious, frantic, raving mad...".[307]

Bloodletting was prescribed for nearly all ailments from a simple cough to small pox.[308]

Folding lancet
with horn handle
Photographed by the author
with permission from
The Colonial Williamsburg Foundation

Diet was a top priority in the military hospital. Munro recorded the following diets allowed in his hospital in Germany between 1761 and 1763:

<u>Full diet:</u>

Breakfast: One pint of rice gruel, made with two ounces of rice, one spoonful of fine flower, a little common salt, and fine sugar.

Dinner: One pound of meat.

Supper: As breakfast.

<u>Middle Diet:</u>

Breakfast: As above.

Dinner: One pint of broth, half a pound of meat.

Supper: As above.

<u>Low Diet:</u>

Breakfast: As above or according to the patient's stomach.

Dinner: One pint of broth or half a pint of Panado, with two spoonfuls of wine, and a quarter of an ounce of sugar.

Supper: Same as breakfast.[309]

Of course, these were the ideal rations, and were subject to availability.

31
REGIMENT

32
REGIMENT

33
REGIMENT

According to Munro, *"Every sick man sent to the general hospital, cost the government at least sixteen pence per day"*.[310] To help pay for the hospital's stores, upkeep, and nurses, every soldier had four pence or more deducted from his pay for each day he spent in the hospital:

"It is customary for all Soldiers while they are sick in the Hospital to have stoppages from their pay, for expence of Nurses, &c.".[311]

Guards were posted to the hospital, and every night the doors, if any, were locked. An NCO or officer inspected the hospital at least once every day. Any patient wishing to leave the hospital required a ticket signed by the head physician. Men that died in the hospital were buried immediately, and had their clothing smoked in a smokehouse, aired, and cleaned before being placed in the regimental stores.[312] According to one soldier, the cost of making a coffin was six shillings six pence, and the cost of digging a grave was five shillings.[313] Every year, a receipt listing burial expenses was given to the Paymaster General, who fronted the bill, or as in the Virginia Regiment in 1755, the dead men remained on the muster roll long enough for their pay to cover the expense of their burials:

"If any non-commissioned Officer or Soldier should happen to die, he is to be continued on the pay-roll as an effective man, for twenty-eight days, to pay for his Coffin, &c.".[314]

Private soldiers and campfollowers often did duty as hospital nurses. If any campfollower refused to serve as a nurse, or neglected that duty, they could expect to be severely punished, as Wolfe stated in August of 1759:

"If any woman refuses to serve as a nurse in the hospitals, or after being there Leaves it without being regularly dismissed by order of the director, shall be struck of[f] the provision roll, and if found afterwards in any of the camps, shall be turned out immediately".[315]

Long voyages aboard ship could prove a serious health hazard where the men were subjected to rolling decks, cramped quarters, bad sanitation, and stale food and water. The best preservatives for the men's health aboard ship, according to General Wolfe, was to *"be as much in the open air as possible, and to eat upon deck, Cleanliness in the berths and bedding, and as much exercise as the situation permits"*.[316] Ship's decks were regularly scrubbed with vinegar and fumigated by burning tarred rope or rosin.[317] When the weather turned cold, extra ship's blankets and bedding were provided for each man, and fires were built inside metal pots or small stoves. Fish were often caught over the sides of the boat to supplement the men's diet.[318]

Opposite
Grenadiers, 31st, 32nd, 33rd Regiments of Foot, 1751
by David Morier
The Royal Collection © 2007
Her Majesty Queen Elizabeth II

Right
Surgeon's etui
dyed rayskin covered wood, inscribed:
"Joseph Hooper, Surgeon, 1754"
Photographed by the author
with permission from
The Colonial Williamsburg Foundation

On The March

Before an army struck camp, the soldier's rations were prepared for the march and issued out:

"This day all the Bakers in the Army where Called to Bake Biskake for the march. We Rec'd three days Provisions".[319]

Great care was taken that all garbage pits and latrines were buried, camp kitchens filled in, huts demolished, and the camp was clean before the army departed; this insured that the military camp would not negatively affect the local community and that the site would be suitable should the need arise to use it again. The tents were struck and loaded onto wagons, or if no wagons were available, the tent, poles, pegs, tools, and other equipment belonging to each mess were equally divided between its members and carried by hand:

"Upon a March the Soldiers are not to hang to their Firelock any Bundle or Kettle, but are to carry them on their Back tied with good strong Straps, The Six Men of each Mess Carrying their Kettles by Turn, as likewise their Tent Poles in their Hands and Tent Pins tied to a String".[320]

Opposite
"An Encampment of British Troops under the command of the Duke of Cumberland"
by David Morier
The Royal Collection © 2007
Her Majesty Queen Elizabeth II

Musket sling buckle
c. 1750-1780
shown actual size
Collection of the
Fort Ticonderoga Museum

Morier's *"An Encampment of British Troops under the command of the Duke of Cumberland"* (seen opposite) shows many details of the soldier's camp and mode of transportation. Soldiers are setting up tents in the background. Some tent poles are standing unsupported suggesting the bottoms may be spiked. The long rows of soldier's tents sit behind the much larger officer's marqees. The foreground shows a row of wagons painted light blueish/gray with canvas covers. A woman with child sits atop a horse laden with goods. It is possible that this woman is a sutler. A cannon is being pulled using a two wheeled "limber" with four horses.

Every soldier was issued a knapsack to carry their clothing and belongings in. These pouches were made from the hides of cows, goats, or other animals, and worn on the back with a single leather strap (see pages 57 and 120).

The weight carried by a grenadier on the march was estimated by Lieutenant Baillie of the 60th Regiment in 1762 at 63 ¾ pounds, which broke down as follows:

"Regimental coat with hooks, eye & ca. 5 lb. 2 Qrs.
Waistcoat, 2 lb. 1 Qrs.
Pair of breeches, 1 lb. 2 Qrs.
Hat with cockade, button, loop & hair string, 1 lb.
A shirt with sleeve buttons, 1 lb.
A stock with a buckle, A pair of knee buckles, A pair of stockings & garters 3 Qrs.
A pair of shoes with buckles, 1 lb. 2 Qrs.
A regimental firelock with a sling & buckle, hammer cap & stopper, 11lb. 1 Qrs.
A waist belt with a buckle, 2 Qrs.
A hanger, sword knot, and scabbard, 2 lb. 3 Qrs.
A Bayonet with Scabbard, 1 lb. 1 Qrs.
A tomahawk, and cover, 1 lb. 3 Qrs.
A cartridge pouch with belt, buckles, & match case, 3 lb.
Containing 24 cartridges, 2 lb. 1 Qrs.
A brush & wire, worm, turnkey, oil bottle, rag, 2 flints & a steel, 1 Qrs.
A knapsack with strap and buckle, 1 lb. 2 Qrs.
Containing 2 shirts, 2 stocks, 2 pairs of stockings, 2 lb. 3 Qrs.
A pair summer breeches, 1 lb. 1 Qrs.
A pair shoes, 1 lb. 1 Qrs.
A clothes brush, pair shoe brushes, blackball, 1 lb.
A pair leggings & garters, a handkerchief, 1 lb. 1 Qrs.
2 combs, a knife & spoon, 2 Qrs.
A haversack with a strap, 3 Qrs.
Containing six days provisions, 10 lb. 1 Qrs.
A blanket with strap & garters, 3 lb. 2 Qrs.
A canteen with a string & stopper, full of water, 3 lb. 1 Qrs.".[321]

Regiments marched in order of seniority (the lower the number being the more senior), with the grenadier company marching at the head of each regiment. When on the march, soldiers were allowed to wear their accouterments and weapons in any fashion most comfortable to them. Waistbelts could be worn around the shoulder, and muskets slung or clubbed (see page 79). Neckstocks could be removed, and possibly the coats as well. The sides of the cocked hat could be let down to shade the face and neck.

34
REGIMENT

35
REGIMENT

36
REGIMENT

To lessen the burden of carrying the wooden tent poles, soldiers sometimes tied them to their muskets, which could then be slung over their shoulders. However, being attacked on the march in this fashion could have disastrous effects, as Bland recorded:

"The Partisans, with eighty horse, rushed out upon them…The men having their tent-poles fastened to their firelocks could make little resistance".[322]

In 1755, Robert Orme recorded an order specifically banning the practice in his journal:

"No man, upon the March, is on any account to fasten his tent pole, to his firelock, or by any means encumber it".[323]

James Wolfe recommended that his soldiers not drink much on the march. Besides preserving the men's health by preventing them from drinking unclean water, this practice kept the soldiers from falling out of the ranks to fetch it, which was preferably done under the supervision of a non-commissioned officer. However, this practice may have caused many cases of dehydration.

"It is recommended to the soldiers not to drink much water upon the march, and the Officers commanding divisions are not to allow men to drink from standing pools, or any kind of dirty water".[324]

Discipline was traditionally relaxed on the march to lessen the burden on the fatigued men. Soldiers were allowed to talk freely, and sometimes even converse with their officers. The conduct of marching soldiers was colorfully depicted in Henry Fielding's 1749 novel "Tom Jones":

"Much mirth and festivity passed among the soldiers during their march. In which the many occurrences that had passed at their last quarters were remembered, and every one, with great freedom, made what jokes he pleased on his officers, some of which were of the coarser kind, and very near bordering on scandal".[325]

Opposite
Grenadiers, 34th, 35th
and 36th Regiments of Foot, 1751
by David Morier
*The Royal Collection © 2007
Her Majesty Queen Elizabeth II*

Marching in the heat of summer with full clothing, accouterments, and little or bad water, could have ill effects on the soldier's health, or could even lead to death, as William Hervey recorded in his journal in July of 1755:

"We had every day violent hot weather, by which the Major lost a man on the march the night before".[326]

Wagons often followed marching armies, which were either brought over from Britain by the Board of Ordnance, or procured locally. A return of the wagons that arrived at Fort Ligonier from Fort Bedford in 1759 included 57 *"kings waggons"*, 19 *"kings drawn by train hors's"*, and 174 *"contracted waggons"*.[327]

Four wheeled wagons and two wheeled tumbrils were widely used, and were often covered with plain or painted canvas covers. Wagons were used to haul everything including food, tools, tents, ammunition, and wounded soldiers. Like the wagons, the drivers were either brought over from Britain or hired locally. "Batmen" were often hired to tend to and drive the horses of the army, as Colonel Bouquet recorded in his orderly book in June of 1758:

"The Bautmen are to take care of the Horses belonging to their Company, load and Drive them upon a March, lead them to the Pasture and tie them every Night in the Camp according to the Orders given".[328]

Batmen were hired from local civilians, freed slaves, and other men. Batmen wore their own clothing, though extra clothing was sometimes provided by the local province. While in Williamsburg in 1755, General Braddock wrote:

"…There are here numbers of mulattoes and free Negroes of whom I shall make Batmen, whom the province are to furnish with pay and frocks, being resolv'd to allow none out of the troops".[329]

After every third day of marching, the troops typically halted for a day to rest. A sailor following Braddock's army in the spring of 1755 recorded:

"As it is customary in the Army to halt a day after 3 days march, we halted to-day to rest the Army".[330]

The quartermasters and camp colour men of each regiment marched ahead of the army to find a suitable location for that night's camp. When a site was found, it was measured and laid it out in preparation for the arrival of the main body.

"A View of the Church of Notre-Dame de la Victoire", Quebec, 1761. Richard Short
Library and Archives Canada, Acc. No. 1989-283-12

Garrison Life

Soldiers did not always live in tents; in fact, a good deal of their enlistment was spent living indoors, be it in a military barracks, lodged in taverns, inns, or billeted in private homes:

"In time of Peace, Soldiers are quartered either in Towns or Garrisons, which they are under the Eye of their Officers, who take Care that they keep themselves clean, and provided with Necessaries; they lie either in private houses or in Barracks, where they have a good Bed, regular Meals of wholesome Provisions, and enjoy most of the other Necessities of Life".[331]

Large cities, port towns, fortresses, and other key locations throughout the empire where large numbers of soldiers were regularly posted required permanent facilities to house them; the military barracks was the answer. The building, supplying, and overseeing of all barracks fell to the Board of Ordnance:

"Our new garrison consisted of…a store-keeper from a board or committee, and constitutes the civil branch of this garrison: they derive their authority from the respectable board of ordnance at home, and under their inspection are the works, barracs, arsenals, stores of various kinds, armoury, and the superintendance as well as payment of all the artificers, and others employed in the King's works, in like manner as in all his Majesty's other forts & garrisons".[332]

Barracks were built using soldier labor under the direction of military engineers. A barracks generally consisted of a simple wooden or stone building, often two storied, with rooms filled with rows of bunks, a fire place, and the occasional window. The bunks sometimes held mattresses stuffed with straw, and were often large enough to hold two or more men. Barracks rooms contained racks for holding muskets, and pegs for hanging accouterments where they could easily be accessed and kept off the floor away from vermin.

Unlike in camp, furniture such as tables, chairs, and benches could be found in a barracks, as well as regular utensils such as earthenware plates, tin cups, clay jugs, wooden bowls, knives, forks, spoons, pots, pans, and lanterns. Colonel Bouquet wrote the following description of a barracks in New York in July of 1757:

"In New York they have built two-story brick barracks with very good rooms, with chimneys and a window. They are furnished with beds, tables, benches, and necessary utensils for the soldier's kitchens".[333]

English made
saltglazed stoneware plate, c. 1740-1760
Private American collection

Fork and pewter spoon, c. 1750-1780
Collection of the Fort Ticonderoga Museum

Bouquet described the barracks in New York again in December of 1758:

"The city of New York have built very comfortable Barrks & furnish'd them with clean bedding, with a large wooden boul and three platters for each mess. Each room has a large table & sufficient number of wooden forms for the whole men of the room to sit on at the same time. The town furnishes two loads (half a chord) of wood every week to each fire place & candles for the guard room".[334]

Each barracks was supervised by a barracks master whose duty was to maintain the barrack's utensils, furniture, and equipment, as well as issue out the soldier's rations, firewood, and candles. It was not uncommon for a barracks to maintain a blacksmith to make and mend door hinges, locks, and other ironwork, or a tinsmith to fix lanterns and cooking pots.

Most barracks rooms had a fireplace for cooking and warmth. Every fireplace was allowed three quarters of a chord of wood every two days.[335] Most barracks and fortresses had clay brick ovens for baking large amounts of bread for the garrison and to supply campaigning armies. Regiments or companies often had to take turns using the ovens, as mentioned in this order given out at Crown Point in 1759:

"The provincials Regiments may use the large Ovens in the Fort; they must here-after serve for Bakeing for all the Corps here...each Corps keeping an Oven 12 Hours and no longer, as each Oven is capable of bakeing 900 Loaves of 6 Pounds in 12 Hours; the small Ovens is for the Artillery and Hospitall".[336]

The largest barracks in Britain were found at Portsmouth, Woolwich, Chatham, and Fort George.[337] When the ranks of the army swelled in times of war, more barracks needed to be built, but throughout the 18th century, there was never a satisfactory number to house every soldier, and many soldiers had to make do with tents.

When the winter weather froze over the lakes and rivers, the roadways became impassible with snow, and it became too cold to live in tents, the campaign season ended and the soldiers went into winter quarters. The barracks, if any, were filled to capacity, and the remaining soldiers were billeted in private homes and businesses in nearby towns. This practice was strictly regulated by Parliament's annual Mutiny Act which helped to preserve the rights of the citizens. No soldiers could be quartered in any private home without the consent of the owner, unless in an emergency, and every home or business owner had to be compensated for

Businesses selected by the Mutiny Act for billeting soldiers included *"Inns, Livery Stables, Ale-houses, Victualling-houses, and the houses of sellers of Wine by Retail...and all houses of persons selling Brandy, Strong Waters, Cyder, or metheglin, by retail".*[338] It was the local parish constable's job to acquaint the officers of the residences willing to lodge the king's men, and the businesses required to do so. Four days warning was supposed to be given to those assigned to house solders. No constable or officer was permitted to take money for excusing any person's home or business liable to house soldiers, though the constables were reluctant to billet soldiers in the houses of the *"...Squire, Parson, Gentleman, or able Farmer...".*[339] Any victualler refusing to quarter soldiers or provide them with sufficient supplies as specified by the Mutiny Act had to pay a fine of between forty shillings and five pounds.[340]

Those citizens or business owners who lodged soldiers were paid by the government to provide the men with *"Candles, Vinegar, and Salt, and with either Small Beer or Cyder, not exceeding five pints for each man per Diem, gratis, and allow to such non-commission Officers or Soldiers the use of fire, and the necessary utensils for dressing and eating their Meat".*[341] The rate for lodging a private soldier in the year 1758 was four pence a day.[342] No inn or victualler was to allow any soldier to contract debts beyond what the government paid for their sustenance.

Tin cup
c. 1758-1766
*Courtesy Fort Ligonier,
Ligonier, Pennsylvania*

Colonel Bouquet described the living conditions of the 60th Regiment quartered in Philadelphia in 1757:

"Everywhere they had good rooms, with chimneys, necessary utensils and beds with a straw mattress on which there was a woolen blanket, sheets, and a pillow, with a second blanket for covering, independent of the beer, fire, salt, etc., specified in the act of parliament".[343]

For a list of the "necessary utensils" issued to the soldiers in quarters, we again turn to Bouquet, who left us a detailed description of the equipment issued to a portion of his soldiers in March of 1758:

"The soldiers who were not Billeted on Public-Houses, were Lodged in convenient Houses hired for that purpose, & properly furnished with necessarys and utensils as follows:

To each room: 1 pot, 1 Broom frying pan, 1 tub or box to carry out the dirt, 1 ladle, 1 long table & 2 forms (benches), *1 flesh fork, 2 platters, 1 trivet or pot hook, 2 bowls & 12 trenchers, 1 pair dog irons, 2 pitchers & 2 mugs, 1 shovel, 1 hatchet, 1 pair tongs, 1 candlestick, 2 chamber pots, A rack for the men's arms & wodden pegs to hang their knapsacks, haversacks, cloaths & ca.*

For every 2 men: One bedstead, 1 bed, 1 bolster, 3 blankets, and a reasonable proportion of wood, candles, small beer, pepper, salt, & vinegar".[344]

When not enough public or private houses were available to quarter all of the soldiers, they were lodged in churches, barns, warehouses, and other available empty spaces. Though they had a roof over their heads, it was sometimes not enough:

"The [First Highland] *Battalion landed the 3d of September with only 16 Sick Men, and were Quartered in a Half finished Church without windows, in Damp Store-houses upon the Quay, and empty Houses where most of the men were obliged to ly upon the Ground without straw or any sort of Covering…the Regiment lost near 60 Men in less than three Months, still greater Numbers must have perish'd if some of the Inhabitants of this Town had not out of Compassion received near 200 of them into their houses".*[345]

Strict regulations were imposed on the soldiers while in quarters, which were often posted inside each barracks or quarter.[346] No soldier was allowed to change rooms with another without permission from his company commander. When a soldier entered his quarters wet, he was always *"to take off his spatterdashes and change his shoes and stockings".*[347] Accouterments and knapsacks were always to be hung up on pegs so they could be retrieved without the least confusion, and to prevent them from being damage by rats or mice. Likewise, the hats were to always be hung up, possibly as Cuthbertson suggested, with the hind flaps facing downwards to preserve their shape.[348] Every day, the beds were made, the floors swept, and the utensils cleaned:

"They (NCOs) *are likewise to see the men keep the caserns or barracs very clean and in good order, and that the utensils belonging to them are never spoiled nor lost... they are to make the men sweep their rooms very clean every morning, and make their beds".*[349]

Before any man could leave their room, they were to dress in a *"soldier-like way"* by *"having their shoes well blacked, their stockings and cravats well rolled, their hat cocked, their hair dressed, and their clothes brushed and put on to the best advantage".*[350] Soldiers were never to appear in town without their swords or bayonets, as according to Cuthbertson, it was *"unsoldier-like"* to be seen without a sidearm.[351]

Bottle
c. 1758-1766
*Courtesy Fort Ligonier,
Ligonier, Pennsylvania*

Bottle stopper
c. 1758-1766
*Courtesy Fort Ligonier,
Ligonier, Pennsylvania*

The quarters were inspected for cleanliness every morning by an NCO, and typically a second time after the beating of tattoo to see that the soldiers were in their quarters:

"They (NCO's) *must go through every room immediately after tat-too, and oblige the men to put out their fires and candle, and go to bed".*[352]

Captains visited their men's quarters at least once a week, and sub-alterns at least twice a week. To keep track of the men, their names were recorded along with their street address or barracks room number.[353] The jobs of the officers and NCO's were made increasingly difficult while the men were in quarters. A considerable amount of their time was spent inspecting the men and their quarters, which could be spread out over a wide area. The men were also more susceptible to laziness and overindulging themselves in what the towns had to offer, as Knox explains:

"...it is impossible to have troops altogether so alert in quarters as in tents: for soldiers cannot take those indulgences in camp which they may be too much induced to do in their barracks where their bedding & c. lie convenient for them. In the next place, by the extensivness of the garrison, men could not be so soon assembled upon sudden emergency, as in a compact incampment...".[354]

Gaming and gambling frequently occurred in quarters, as the men had more free time and were not observed as closely by their officers. In response, Colonel Joseph Frye, commander of the garrison at Fort Cumberland in September of 1759, issued the following order to his men:

"Whereas I have been Inform'd the non Commissd. Officers and private Soldiers have accustomed themselves to gameing at Cards in ye Barracks Which keeps them up Late in the night Which Of Course Unfitts them for Duty and is Likely may be the means of Leaving their fires in such a Careless manner as to Endanger their Burning the Barracks therefore all Such Gameing is forbidden and the Officers are hereby Enjoyn'd to Use their Utmost Endeavours to supress the same".[355]

Officers were generally quartered in public and private houses near their soldiers, and were allowed multiple rooms, depending on their rank, at the rate of three rooms for each field officer, two rooms for each captain, and one room for each subaltern.[356] Officer's quarters were sometimes chosen by drawing lots in order to *"avoid shewing partiality".*[357] The rates paid to lodge officers under the rank of captain was one shilling a day, plus six pence for every horse to pay for hay and straw.[358]

Case bottle
c. 1758-1766
Courtesy Fort Ligonier,
Ligonier, Pennsylvania

Opposite
Grenadiers, 37th, 38th
and 39th Regiments of Foot, 1751
by David Morier
The Royal Collection © 2007
Her Majesty Queen Elizabeth II

37
REGIMENT

38
REGIMENT

39
REGIMENT

Winter Clothing and Accouterments

During the winter months, when campaigning was put to a halt by frozen river and snow covered roads, the soldier's life continued; guards needed to be posted, wood had to be cut, and scouts had to be sent to observe the enemy. Soldiers living in houses or barracks were not to rely solely on fireplaces or stoves for warmth, but were to rely on warm clothing.[359] A regimental coat sometimes proved adequate, as the lapels could be buttoned across the chest for warmth, the cuffs rolled down to protect the hands, and the tails let down to protect the thighs. Private soldiers were not issued extra winter clothing as part of their yearly allotment, but were issued extra clothing, if needed, at the onset of winter, and returned it at its conclusion.

Warm clothing was shipped from Britain to the troops abroad, or was simply purchased from clothiers near the regiment. During an English or European winter, a soldier might receive an extra pair of stockings, an extra waistcoat or breeches, an additional blanket, and a pair of mittens. In America, the clothing was often modeled after that of the French-Canadians and Indians who had adapted so well to the severe climate. French Canadian blanket coats or "capotes" were common, as well as leather Indian moccasins, fur caps, and wool leggings. The soldier's old clothing was sometimes turned into mittens, stockings, or caps. General Forbes' list of necessary winter clothing in 1758 included *"...a second blanket in lieu of a bed, A flannel jacket, A new pair of breeches, two pair of stockings, and a pair of shoes"*.[360] In November of 1759, Captain Knox recorded that each man was issued *"one pair of leggens, one pair of spare shoes, one pair of good spare stockings, one warm waistcoat, one good blanket, and one pair of warm mittens"*,[361] and Colonel Bouquet in the same year proposed to *"Equip each soldier, besides his uniform, with an overcoat, made from a blanket, or at least a flannel jacket, two pairs of good stockings, two pairs of new shoes, some prepared skins to supply the "woodsmen" with moccasins, a pair of leggings, a cap made of blanketing and some mittens"*.[362]

As the grenadier's caps offered little protection against the cold, they were sometimes allowed to wear hats when mounting guard or performing other duties during the winter, as William Hervey recorded in December of 1762:

"The Grenadiers during the winter are to mount guard with hats".[363]

Knox described in detail how leggings were constructed in 1758:

"Leggers, Leggins, or Indian spatterdashes are usually made of frize, or other course wollen cloth; they should be at least three quarters of a yard in length; each leggin about three quarters wide (which is three by three) then double it, and sew it together from end to end, within four, five, or six inches of the outside selvages. Fitting this long narrow bag to the shape of the leg, the flaps to be on the outside, which serve to wrap over the skin, or forepart of the legs, tied round under the knee and above the ankle, with garters of the same color by which the legs are preserved from many fatal accidents...The army have made an ingenious addition to them by putting a tongue or sloped piece before, as there is in the lower part of a spatterdash, and a strap fixed to it under the heart of the foot which fastens under the outside ankle with a button".[364]

Major John Tulleken of the 60th Regiment in a letter to Colonel Bouquet described the leggings worn by his men in 1759:

"Our people have leggings. I intended always that the should have been Blue, but we could not have blue at Albany, so that we have green, tied with a red Garter".[365]

It is possible that leggings were preferred to be made in the same color as a regiments facings; that certainly seems to be the case for the 60th Regiment who had blue facings and breeches, as noted by Major Tulleken in 1760:

"As to the Leggins wee are of opinion here, if it is agreeable to you, that Blue will be the best Colour because when the campaign is over, and if they are made properly large, they make good breeches, and uniform with the cloathing".[366]

Soldier's wore anything and everything they could to keep warm, which altered their normally uniform appearance, as Knox described in a December journal entry:

"Our guards on the Grand Parade make a most grotesque appearance in their different dresses, and our inventions to guard us against the extreme rigour of this climate are so various beyond imagination: the uniformity as well as nicety of the clean, methodical soldier is buried in the rough fur-wrought garb of the frozen Laplander, and we rather resemble a masquerade than a body of regular troops".[367]

For soldiers whose duties required venturing out during the winter, the deep snow and slippery ice was a serious hazard. To aid soldiers in winter traveling they were issued a variety of tools including iron ice creepers, ice skates, and wooden snowshoes. Knox recorded the following regarding the 43rd Regiment in November of 1759:

"As the regiment will have a number of creepers, snowshoes or rackets, and mogosans delivered to them, they will take care to keep them properly fitted, that they may be come at for use on the shortest notice, the snowshoes to be kept hung up, to prevent the rats and mice from eating them…".[368]

Other soldiers simply wore what they could find:

"…The ground is become so slippery…The troops are obliged to prevent meeting with accident by falling: some wearing coarse stockings over their shoes, with an additional sole or two, of thick frize or other woollen cloth; some wear mogosans, and others again use what are termed creepers ".[369]

Snowshoes, as Knox explains, were made of:

"…hoops of hickory, or other tough wood bended to a particular form, round before, and the two extremities of the hoop terminate in a point behind secured will together with strong twine: The inward space is worked like close netting with cat gut, or the dried entrails of other animals. Each racket is from three quarters to one yard in length at the broadest part, which is about the center where it is fastened by thongs and straps to the person's foot. It is about fourteen, fifteen, or sixteen inches…".[370]

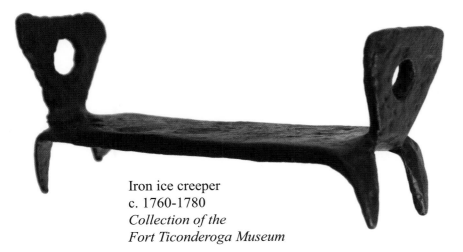

Iron ice creeper
c. 1760-1780
*Collection of the
Fort Ticonderoga Museum*

Soldiers practiced walking in their snowshoes, which was very fatiguing for those unaccustomed to it:

"The commanding officers of regiments are desired to make their light infantry practice walking on snow shoes, preparatory to the service for which they are reserved…some of Captain Hazen's New England Rangers are appointed to instruct our soldiers in the use of them".

"Our soldiers make great progress in walking on snow-shoes, but men not accustomed to them fund them very fatiguing…".

"The Light Infantry are ordered to do no more duties of fatigue, and to practice walking on snow-rackets from morning until evening".[371]

Hard soled shoes were not suitable for snowshoes, as they easily damaged the gut webbing; instead, the snowshoes were worn with leather moccasins. Moccasins were so helpful in preventing slipping, frostbite, and wear on their regular shoes, that in December of 1759, every soldier in the 43rd Regiment was ordered to wear them for all future duties:

"The mogosans which have been delivered to the Quartermaster are to be issued to the men Immediately, as they are only useful in the frost, and were provided with a view not only to prevent the soldiers being frost-bitten, but to save their shoes; it is therefore expected that no soldier parade for the future without them for any duty whatsoever".[372]

Even with the additional clothing, frostbite was a common occurrence in winter, which particularly affected the men's noses, ears, and fingers. Knox recorded the following as one doctor's remedy for frost bite in 1759:

"Doctor Russel recommends, that every person to who this accident may happen should be particularly careful to avoid going near a fire, and to have the part front-bitten rubbed with snow by one who has a warm hand, and, as soon as can be, afterwards put into a blanket, or something of that kind, that will restore heat to the part".[373]

"The Town and Harbour of Halifax, Nova Scotia", 1764. Richard Short
Library and Archives Canada, Acc. No. 1970-188-120

Life Aboard Ship

Most soldiers during the course of their service would find themselves at sea. General Wolfe, writing aboard the ship Ramillies in 1757, had this to say of the life:

"...for a man that does not feel the ship's motion, and who's nose is not too nice for the smells, this life for a little while is tolerable".[374]

Ocean transportation fell under the jurisdiction of the Admiralty Board. Instead of maintaining a large fleet of transport ships, the navy simply hired civilian transports and merchant vessels to move troops and ordnance.[375] Transporting soldiers aboard the navy's ships of war was also very common. The main ports for embarking troops were at Portsmouth, Plymouth, and Bristol in England, and Cork in Ireland.[376] Port towns were often bristling with soldiers, either in garrison, or awaiting transportation. These towns offered soldiers every conceivable vice, from gambling and drinking to prostitution. General Wolfe described the effect this had on the soldiers at Portsmouth in 1758:

"...The conditions of the troops that composite this garrison (or rather vagabonds that stroll about in dirty red clothes from one Gin-Shop to another) exceeds all belief, There is not the Least shaddow of Discipline, care, or attention. Disorderly soldiers of different Regiments are collected here, some from ships, others from hospital, some waiting to embark – dirty, drunken, insolent rascals, improved by the hellish nature of the place, where every kind of corruption, immorality, and looseness is carried to excess, it is a sink of the lowest and most abominable of vices".[377]

After boarding ship, the soldiers were issued their "sea bedding" consisting of an extra blanket, pillow, and sometimes a hammock or rug.[378] Eating utensils were also issued to each man consisting of a wooden bowl and spoon. Quarters aboard ship were often very cramped. In one case, as many as ten men were allowed a birth measuring six feet square.[379] Corporal Todd pointed out while on board a transport ship in 1757 that his berth was so small, that of the six men assigned to it, only four could lay down at a time.[380] Soldiers received no money while aboard ship, but were given their "sea pay" after they disembarked as Corporal Todd recorded while crossing the English Channel in September of 1758:

"...Money is very scarce amongst our troops, as we never receive any pay untill we Land, & then we get our sea pay from the time that we Embark'd until the time we return".[381]

Three pence were taken from every man's pay each day spent aboard ship to pay for their rations, which were cut nearly in half.[382] When sailing in hot climate areas, the men's rations of beef and pork, which easily spoiled, were substituted with biscuits, flour, oatmeal, or rice, which lasted longer.[383] To keep track of what type of rations were to be issued, and when, a list was fixed to the ship's mast by the commanding officer.[384] Every day, one man from each mess was excused from his duties to cook the food for his messmates, as Captain Jonathan Eddy recorded in his orderly book in April of 1759:

"Orders sent on Board Every Transport...Orderd that a man be Excus'd from duty out of every Mess to Cook for said Mess".[385]

Soldiers were kept constantly busy while aboard ship. Soldiers mounted as guards throughout the ship to maintain strict order and to prevent fires.[386] Men with previous experience at sea worked along with the sailors. The soldiers sometimes acted as marines, and drilled in the marine fashion upon the quarterdeck and forecastle, which, as Knox explained, *"is nothing more than after firing over the ship's side, to fall down upon one knee, so as to be under cover and load again".*[387] Because of the cramped space aboard the ship's boats, a small landing party of infantry in August of 1757 was issued naval cutlasses instead of muskets.[388]

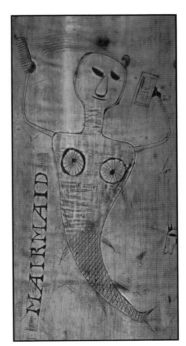

To maintain their health, the men ate and exercised above deck as much as possible.[389] Fishing tackle and nets could usually be found aboard ship, and the men fished over the sides of the boat to supplement their rations. The ship was cleaned constantly. The men's births and bedding were cleaned and aired out daily, and fresh air was pumped between the decks:

"All hands orderd to bring their Beds & Blankets On deck to Air and sweeten them and in order to Clean out the Births...".[390]

"We had also Every Morning half an Hours work pumping the foul Air out & Fresh Air in betwixt the decks...".[391]

Left

Some surviving military powder horns include maritime iconography such as this mermaid.
c. 1756-1770
Jim Dresslar collection

"A General View of Quebec, from Point Levy", 1761. Richard Short
Library and Archives Canada, Acc. No. 1989-283-1

The decks were regularly washed and sprinkled with vinegar. Rosin, frankincense, or tarred rope were burned between decks to fumigate the air.[392] To keep warm, fires were lit in small stoves or iron kettles. Guards were always placed over the fires to prevent accidents.[393]

Soldiers aboard ship were still expected to wash themselves regularly, comb their hair daily, and put on clean linens at least twice a week.[394] It was custom aboard ship for soldiers not on duty to wear their clothing inside out to prevent them from getting dirty, as Knox recorded in June of 1757:

"...our soldiers having white linings to their uniforms, and their cloaths being turned outside in, for cleanliness, according to the custom of troops at sea...".[395]

When the destination was reached, the soldiers disembarked first, followed by their camp equipment, and lastly by the sutlers and campfollowers. The ship's boats were used to transport soldiers from ship to shore and vice-versa, as well as larger flat bottomed boats specifically designed for transporting troops. Friedrich graf von Kielmansegge described the transport boats he saw while visiting England in 1761 and 1762:

"These boats are arranged for fifty to sixty men; their shape is somewhat similar to that of the long boats which men-of-war generally carry but they are much larger, and have flat buttoms for the purpose of getting closer to shore...each of which has twenty to twenty-four oars".[396]

Von Kielmansegge further recorded the method in which the troops embarked on these boats:

"The officers and drummers, with their corporals, sit aft near the rudder, the privates in two or three rows behind one another on the thwarts, holding their muskets before them, and two petty officers sit in the bows, but the oarsmen occupy especial rows between the soldiers, and a little in front of them, so as not to be hampered in the use of the oars. As soon as everything has been arranged in this way, the naval officer commanding the embarkation gives a signal, when all the boats start off at the same time and row their respective vessels".[397]

British sailors. Detail taken from:
"A View of the Church of Notre-Dame de la Victoire"
Quebec, 1761. Richard Short
Library and Archives Canada, Acc. No. 1989-283-12

British naval cutlass
with leather scabbard
c. 1755-1760
Courtesy Col. J. Craig Nannos

4ᵗ
REGIMENT

INVALIDS
REGIMENT

42.
REGIMENT

In addition to muskets, highland soldiers were issued basket-hilted swords, a style of sword popular in the highlands. While most regiments were ordered to leave their swords behind on campaign, highland regiments were often exempt:

"Soldiers carry no sword or sword belt if they can carry their Bayonet securely without them...The Royal Highlanders and the 77th are exempted in the order of no swords".[415]

The swords, traditionally made in Scotland, were purchased by the colonels from cutlers in England at a cheaper rate. The sword's steel basket protected the hand from sword cuts, and could also be used as an offensive weapon. The hilts were decorated with geometric piercing, which besides making the them more attractive, also made them lighter. The wooden handles were wrapped with shagreen, the texture of which made a perfect grip, and were secured by a wrapping of twisted wire. The length of the blades varied, but were usually between 32 and 36 inches long. A return of the swords in the Tower of London in 1756 included:

"Highlanders' swords; hilts of the same pattern, but blades of different patterns:

36 inches 25
35 ½ inches 44
34 ½ inches 87
34 inches 172
33 ½ inches 60
33 inches 95
32 ½ inches . . . . . 85" [416]

The sword blades were often stamped with the maker's mark, and the hilts engraved with the soldier's number, and the letter of their company. Captain Stewart recorded in April of 1759:

"The three Companys here of the 2nd Battn to have their swords numbrd and lettred as soon as possible beginning with the letter "L" the 1st Bn having ended with the letter "K.".[417]

Sword scabbards were made of black leather, with brass or iron tips, and were secured in the sword belt with a metal hook or finial located near the top. The sword belts were made of black leather, with brass or iron buckles, and were worn over the right shoulder, hanging over the left hip.

One, or sometimes two pistols were issued to the soldiers of highland regiments. These distinctly Scottish style pistols were smaller than those used by officers or cavalry, and were made entirely of metal, with belt hooks, and no triggerguards. The pistol was worn under the left arm, hung by the pistol's belt hook on a leather strap around the right shoulder. Highland officers carried similar pistols, though more elaborately decorated. This style of pistol was very popular with the Scottish gentry, who often wore highly decorated versions (sometimes not even functional) as a sort of jewelry. Scottish pistols, traditionally made by the Murdochs, Campbells, and other Scottish gunsmithing families in cities like Edinburgh and Stirling, were made cheaply for the army in Birmingham, England.[418]

The American campaigns of 1758-59 saw distinct alterations in the uniforms and weapons of the highland regiments, resulting from the rough country, severe climate, and the guerrilla tactics of the French and their Indian allies. Around 1758, the 42nd Regiment began wearing "philabegs", or "kilts", which were made by sewing the pleats on old plaids and removing the excess drappage. Kilts were much lighter, easier to maintain, and faster to put on. By 1759, they were in common use:

"The Non Commissioned Officers and men are at all times in Camp to wear their kelts except when otherwise ordered".[419]

"The men to appear for the future when under arms in kelt or felebeggs".[420]

Besides plaids and kilts, the men of the 42nd Regiment were also issued canvas breeches for fatigue duties:

"The Commanding Officers of Companies to review the state of mens britches and new britches to be immediately made up taking care that those who are most needful be first provided. The pattern will be seen with a man of Major Reids Company".[421]

"A return to be given in of the number of britches that are made in each company as also of a pattern waistcoat and leggans as made according to former orders as it is suppose that those who wear most in want in britches are supplied. They may be permitted to wear them at work therefore no man is to go to work with his plaid".[422]

Officer's basket hilted broadsword
c. 1730-1750
Private collection

Wool Indian leggings began to be worn in lieu of the tartan hose, as they offered better protection for the legs and shoes. The leggings were most likely supported using the same red tape garters that supported the hose:

"The men to be completed as soon as possible in leggans and fellewbeggs sufficient at least for 3 months wear".[423]

The 42nd Regiment, and possibly others, were issued Indian "tumplines", which were long straps of leather or woven material, the ends of which were tied around the men's blanket rolls. This allowed the blankets to be worn slung over the shoulder:

"The Regimt to be under arms on Wednesday morning with their Linen britches and leggans and packs tied up properly with their toplines".[424]

The light infantry companies of highland regiments were dressed and accoutered according to the regulations issued by General Amherst,[425] though they retained their bonnets. Breeches may have been worn by the light companies in lieu of kilts. As light infantry, the highlanders replaced their swords with tomahawks and left their pistols in storage.

Scottish steel pistol
made by Alexander Forbes
Elgin, Scotland, c. 1740-1750
*Collection of the
Fort Ticonderoga Museum*

Overall length: 11.5"
Barrel length: 6.61"
Caliber: 0.62

Many highlanders were quick to adapt to military life. The 77th and 78th Highland Regiments were sent to America comprised of *"...young soldiers, being raw and unexperienced, and very few of them conversant in, or able to talk English..."*.[426] Wolfe had this to say of them only a year later:

"The Highlanders are very useful serviceable soldiers, and commanded by the most manly corps of officers I ever saw".[427]

Highland officers, 78th Regiment
detail taken from:
*"A View of the Cathedral,
Jesuits College, and Recollet Friars
Church, taken from the Gate of the
Governor's House"*. Quebec, 1761
Richard Short
*Library and Archives Canada,
Acc. No. 1989-283-7*

Pioneers, Camp Colour Men, and Musicians

Not every soldier's duty was solely to fight. Each battalion had a detachment of "pioneers" who acted as a permanent labor detail. The pioneer detail was made up of one man from each battalion company, with a corporal in command. Overall command of the pioneers and their corporals fell to the quartermaster. The duties performed by pioneers included cutting trees and brush, clearing ground for camps, gathering and cutting firewood, building bridges, making fascines, gabions, and chevaux de frise, constructing and mending roads, setting up tents, and burying the dead.[428] Pioneers were exempt from regimental duties, as Corporal Todd stated while commanding the pioneers of the 12th Regiment in 1761:

"...I was to deliver to Each man his tools, & for me to take there Names down & the company they belong'd too, each man, that was Appointed by his Captain for that Duty, & that we were not to be order'd upon any Duty with the Regiment during the Campaign".[429]

Captains hand picked the men from their companies to be pioneers, typically choosing men of considerable strength. Todd wrote in June of 1761.

"I Order'd all my Pioneers to the right of the Regiment with Orders for them to perade there for the future, & the Officers said that we were all a set of strong built men, very Sizable & fit for that station".[430]

When more than one battalion was present, the pioneers from each battalion often brigaded together:

"...Orders came from the Quartermaster General for all the Pioneers to perade with their tools at the Head of the Hessian Guards in order to Cutt through the wood a road for the Collumns to March. And Accordingly we peraded about 400 pioneers where a party was ready drawn up to Escort us".[431]

The pioneers retained their regimental clothing, with the exception of cloth caps in lieu of cocked hats, and the addition of leather aprons:

"Lieutt Stappleton told me to day that Major Chabbert said that I look'd better under a Pioneers Cap".[432]

Bill hook
c. 1750-1780
Collection of the
Fort Ticonderoga Museum

Pioneer caps were similar to the soldier's fatigue caps, except with a crossed axe and saw decorating the front (see below).[433]

To perform their many duties, pioneers were issued tools such as hatchets, spades, saws, bill hooks, axes, and shovels:

"...the Major Order'd the Quartermaster to deliver to me all the Caps, Aprons, Hatchets & Saws that belong'd the Pioneers out of the store, as we have all new every year...".[434]

Besides their tools, pioneers also carried their muskets, bayonets, and accouterments, as they occasionally had to fight and defend themselves, like Corporal Todd's pioneers in July of 1761:

"...our Drums was Order'd to beat to Arms, & every Pioneer to quit his work & fall into his ranks...Joseph Jacobs, one of my Pioneers, receiv'd a shot in his Belly close by me...".[435]

Part of an engraving after William Hogarth's
"The March to Finchley"
showing a pioneer with cap

The camp colour men also fell under the command of the quartermaster, and often worked together with the pioneers. Bland described the role of the camp colour men in his 1753 treatise:

"There is a sergeant of the regiment and a man from each company, appointed to assist the Quartermaster during the campaign, in making out and keeping the camp clean and healthy; as well as doing all other things that pertains to their duty. These duties are receiving and assisting in the issuing out of all ammunition bread and other species of rations that shale be distributed to the regiment. Also, to assist in the making up and issuing out of all ammunition, working tools, clothes, and accouterments. For this reason they do no other duty but these for the campaign entire".[436]

Another of the camp colour men's duties was the laying out of military encampments. The art of laying out a proper military camp was called "castrametation". Knowing roughly how far the army could march in a day, the camp colour men, quartermaster, and pioneers, set out well ahead of the army to prepare and lay out the next camp:

"And Lieut Barlow, Quartermaster Serjeant Cole & the Camp Collour Men is March'd to Joyn the Other Quartermasters & Camp Collour Men belonging our Brigade to Mark out the ground for our Encampment ready against tomorrow that we get their etc.".[437]

Like the pioneers, the camp colour men from multiple battalions often brigaded together. As the name implies, camp colour men carried with them the camp colors of each regiment, which are described in the 1751 Royal Clothing Warrant:

"The Camp Colours to be Square, and of the Colour of the facing of the Regiment, with the Number of the Regiment upon them".[438]

The camp colours were attached to poles, and were used to mark the boundaries of the company streets to prevent them from intermixing. The individual streets and rows of tents were then measured with rope, or simply by step, and marked using stakes or pieces of wood:

"When we came to our ground, as the old soldiers stiled it, we found several boughs stuck in the earth, as a mark where to fix our tents".[439]

Axe head and shovel, c. 1754
*Jumonville, Braddock Road
Preservation Association*

Camp colour men also performed many laborious duties such as building roads, leveling camp sites, digging kitchens, and more:

"And a man of every company is appointed Camp Colour men, those carrys spades to level the roads under the command of the Quartermaster Serjeant...".[440]

"...the camp-colourmen of the regiment were employed in making cooking places and necessary houses...".[441]

To perform these duties, camp colour men carried tools such as spades, shovels, and hatchets:

"Each camp-colour-man carries either a spade or a hatchet, which are delivered to them from the train".[442]

Nothing extraordinary was worn by the camp colour men to distinguish them from the common soldier. It is possible they wore fatigue caps similar to the pioneers instead of cocked hats.

Musicians were important members of the 18th century army. In camp, the musician's job using their drums, fifes, and bagpipes, was to wake the sleeping soldiers, signal them when it was time to receive rations, stand to arms, and when to bed for the night:

"The Drummer must observe to beat, at the appointed times, the following Beats. Revele at day-break; Troop, at ten o'clock; Retreat at sun-set; and Tattoo, at nine o'clock at night. An Officer is to see that the above Orders are duly executed".[443]

The noise of battle or marching could often obscure the shouts of the officer's orders, thus music was used to signal orders, which could be heard more clearly:

"The Officers and serjeants are to be very attentive to the beat of the drum, taking care always to halt when they hear the long roll beat at the part of the line from which they are detached, and to march upon beating the long march".[444]

Musicians were to practice daily. In July of 1759, Lord Loudoun ordered:

"The Drummers of the line to turn out every evening at the Head of their own Regiment half an hour before gun firing to practice their several Beatings".[445]

Detail taken from:
"An Incident in the Rebellion of 1745"
by David Morier
photographed by Antonia Reeve
*The Royal Collection © 2007
Her Majesty Queen Elizabeth II*

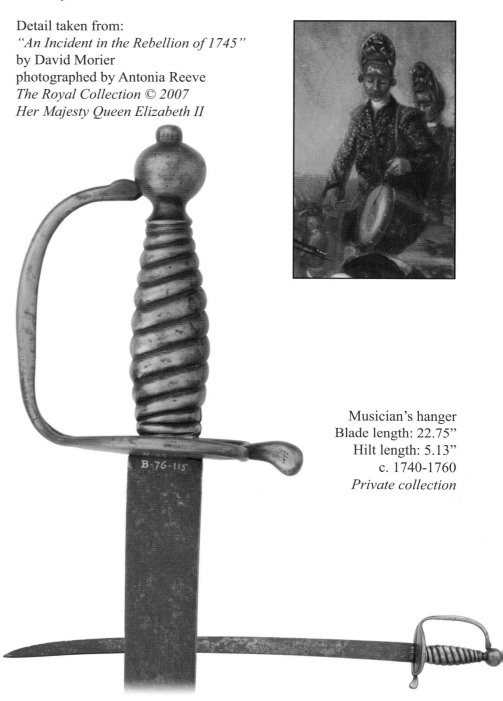

Musician's hanger
Blade length: 22.75"
Hilt length: 5.13"
c. 1740-1760
Private collection

Another job performed by musicians was administering punishment to court-martialed soldiers, commonly in the form of flogging, or lashings with a whip called a "cat-o-nine-tails".[446]

Musician's uniforms were similar in cut as those of the soldiers, but with the coat and facing colors reversed. The color reversal however did not apply to royal regiments as described in the Royal Clothing Warrant of 1751:

"The Drummers of all the Royal Regiments are allowed to wear the Royal Livery, viz., Red. lined, faced, and lapelled on the breast with blue, and laced with Royal lace: The Drummers of all the other Regiments are to be clothed with the Colour of the Facing of their Regiments, lined, faced, and lapelled on the Breast with Red, and laced in such manner as the Colonel shall think fit for distinction sake, the Lace, however, being of the Colours of that on the Soldiers' coats".[447]

Musician's coats had two false sleeves hanging from the shoulders down the back, a vestige of 16th and 17th century fashion (see page 57). The following order dated November 15th, 1751, suggests that these false sleeves may have first been introduced into the Georgian army by the Guards Regiment:

"...the Drummers of the Foot are to have hanging sleeves as the Foot Guards have...".[448]

Musician's wore mitre caps similar to those worn by grenadiers, only shorter, and with a hanging back panel. The 1751 Clothing Warrant does not describe the appearance of infantry drummer caps, but describes those worn by cavalry drummers, which as it states, are similar to those worn by the infantry:

"The Caps of the Drummers to be such as those of the Infantry, with the Tassel hanging behind, the front to be of the colour of their facing with the particular badge of the regiment embroidered on it, or a trophy of guidons and drums, the little flap to be red, with the White Horse and Motto over it, "Nec aspera terrent"; the back part of the Cap to be red likewise; the turn up to be the colour of the front, and in the middle part of it behind, a Drum, and the rank of the regiment".[449]

Later in the same year, the Duke of Cumberland ordered that the infantry drummers *"...are to have caps as is fully explained in the regulations for the Cavalry, only the trophy is to be of Colours & Drums instead of Guidons".[450]*

Occasionally, musicians were issued muskets and fought alongside the other soldiers:

"...General Amherst's orders are that one Drummer in each Company is to Carry Arms, remaining still a Drummer, & being paid & returned as such".[451]

Some colonels paid for their own regimental bands, which performed for the officers and special occasions. The band belonging to the 3rd Regiment, the "Buffs", performed a public concert on December 29th, 1749. Looking at the concert's program, posted in an advertisement in the Sussex Weekly Advisor on December 25th, 1749, gives us an idea of the types of instruments that made up the regimental band:

"At the White Hart in Lewes, next Friday evening, being the 29th of December, will be performed, a Public Concert of Musick, by the Band belonging to his Majesty's Regiment of Buffs, commanded by the Hon. Col. George Howard.

> *Act. I.*
> *1. Symphony with French Horns*
> *2. Hautboy Concerto*
> *3. Violin Concerto*
> *4. Solo for the French Horn*
> *5. Symphony with French Horns*

> *Act. II*
> *1. Symphony with French Horns*
> *2. Hautboy Concerto*
> *3. Solo for the Trumpet*
> *4. German Flute Concerto*
> *5. Symphony with French Horns"* [452]

Non-Commissioned Officers

Non-commissioned officers included corporals, sergeants, sergeant majors, and drum majors. The most junior grade, the corporal, was promoted from the ranks. Each company had three corporals. It was their duty to maintain order and discipline, watch over the men in their company, instruct them in the manual of arms, and teach them every aspect of a soldier's duty. Corporals were paid eight pence per day; two pence more per day than a private soldier. The corporal's uniforms were identical to those of the private men, but with the addition of a "corporal's knot", as mentioned by Corporal Todd:

"...Serjeant William Burnet of our Company was broke by the Majors Orders for being Drunk when he should [have] *Attended the Hospital, the Doctor reported him, & that James Crawford, Corporal, was Appointed Serjeant, & that I was Appointed Corporal in the room of Corporal Crawford prefer'd...I returned home to my Quarters, & Corporal Crawford Cut off his Knott & gave it me to put it upon my coat...".*[453]

Corporal's knots were made of white braided cord or regimental lace, which were worn hanging from the right shoulder.

Every regiment had three sergeants, who were promoted from the pool of corporals, and were paid one shilling a day. The sergeant's role was to oversee the private soldiers and corporals of their company, and act as an intermediate between the common soldiers and officers.

Sergeant's uniforms were often made of higher quality cloth than those of the private soldiers, and were trimmed with plain white lace, or in some regiments, silver or gold lace, in lieu of regimental lace. In 1761, silver and gold lace were banned from being worn by sergeants, exclusive of sergeant majors and drum majors.[454]

A Grenadier sergeant with halberd, sash, and smallsword.
detail taken from:
"An Incident in the Rebellion of 1745"
by David Morier
photographed by Antonia Reeve
The Royal Collection © 2007
Her Majesty Queen Elizabeth II

Opposite
Grenadiers, 43rd, 44th, and 45th Regiments of Foot, 1751
by David Morier
The Royal Collection © 2007
Her Majesty Queen Elizabeth II

Sergeant's smallsword, 23rd Royal Welsh Fusiliers
bronze hilt, wire & tape bound grip , engraved XXIII REG[T.] $\frac{B}{2}$
blade length: 30.25", hilt length: 6.75"
c. 1760-1770
Private collection

A sash was worn around the waist, woven in scarlet wool, with a stripe running through the middle in the color of the regiment's facings. Some sergeants had wool cloaks or great coats for bad weather:

"Sergeants are always to wear Swords, they are not to put on their great Coats between beating and Tatoo unless the weather should be remarkably bad…".[455]

A style of pole axe called a "halberd" was carried by sergeants, which was both a symbol of rank, and a tool used for maneuvering soldiers. In America, sergeants often left their bulky halberds in storage and drew muskets and bayonets, as these passages from 1755 and 1759 state:

"The Sergents of the two Regiments (44th & 48th) are to be provided with Firelocks and Bayonets, but to wear their Swords".[456]

"The serjeants to carry firelocks instead of halberts, with carouch box and bayonet instead of sword".[457]

Sergeants carried hangers or smallswords worn in the frog of their waist-belts. Some sergeants, like those in the 33rd Regiment in 1754, purchased silver mounted swords:

"The Sergeants have a set of silver-mounted swords making up at their own expense".[458]

The sergeant major was the battalion's most senior sergeant whose duty was to watch over and instruct the other sergeants. The drum major's duty was to watch over the regiment's musicians, and teach them the musical signal calls. Upwards of six pence a month was deducted from each drummer, which was paid to the drum major for training the drummers and repairing the drums.[459]

The non-commissioned officer class was a cliquish society, as Corporal Todd observed in 1756:

"Here our Major Chapman gave Orders that no Serjeant should drink with the Corporals nor Corporals to drink with the Private Soldiers nor Soldiers to drink with Drummers neither to keep Company with Each Other but the Serjeant & Corporals to carry sticks & Beat the Soldiers as they so Occation to keep them at a distance in not making themselves so free with them…".[460]

In 1756, the company of the 30th Regiment in which Todd was corporal was further segregated when the sergeants and corporals each started their own exclusive clubs.[461]

Company commanders, who promoted their own NCO's, looked for certain qualifications in their candidates. Men of good stature and figure were preferred. They had to be honest, sober, always neat in their dress and appearance, and masters of the manual of arms.

Sergeants preferably could read and write, as one officer suggested:

"He ought to apply himself to his duty, and be exact in it, also equitable and just in his accounts; for which reason he ought to be Master of Writing and Arithmetick, both for the good of the Service and the Interest of his Captain".[462]

Occasionally, senior NCO's were promoted to the rank of ensign. These promotions were more common when new regiments were raised in times of war, and needed a staff of experienced officers quickly.[463]

Sergeant's halberd, with ash haft
head length: 15.37", width: 8.87"
top blade length: 8.50"
overall length: 8' 1"
c. 1750-1770
Private collection

Commissioned Officers

The British officer class was made up, in part, of gentlemen of wealth, education, or nobility, and elevated non-commissioned officers. Becoming an officer was a considerable investment. Any gentlemen with enough money could simply purchase a commission from the rank of ensign to lieutenant colonel, though every commission had to be approved by both the king and the Secretary-at-War.[464] The government fixed the rate for the sale of commissions, which were as follows:

Lieutenant Colonel: £3,400
Major: £2,500
Captain: £1,500
Captain-Lieutenant: £800
Lieutenant: £550
Ensign: . . . . £400 [465]

To purchase a commission, one had to be above 13 years of age, Protestant, and literate. Commissions were more desirable in older regiments, which were less likely to be disbanded. Newly raised regiments could potentially be disbanded at the end of a conflict.[466] Likewise, commissions in regiments on the English establishment were preferred to those on the Irish establishment, as they were larger and better supplied.[467] Many high ranking officers were wealthy land owners, peers of the realm, or aspiring politicians.[468] However, men with money, titles, or position, did not always make the best officers, as Bland remarked:

"Money and powerful relations will always procure them what they want; they have therefore no occasion to apply themselves to the knowledge of their duty. It is from this way of thinking that so many of them do so little credit to their posts".[469]

Officer with spontoon, c. 1755
Military & Historical Image Bank
www.historicalimagebank.com

Officer's shoe buckle
c. 1758-1766
Courtesy Fort Ligonier,
Ligonier, Pennsylvania

Detachable ruffled shirt cuff
belonging to Captain Thomas Plumbe
1ˢᵗ Royal Lancashire Militia, 1760-1765
Courtesy
King's Own Royal Regiment Museum, Lancaster

Neckstock buckle
c. 1760-1780
shown actual size
Collection of the
Fort Ticonderoga Museum

Officers were not issued their clothing like the rank and file, but had them custom tailored, and purchased with their own funds. The clothing, accouterments, and weapons of the officer class exceeded that of the private soldier in both quality and quantity. The regimental uniforms of the officers conformed to the Royal Clothing Warrant in their cut and facing colors. Though the cut of the uniform was similar to that of a private soldier, officer's uniforms were made of superior quality "superfine" wool, and trimmed with gold or silver metallic lace instead of regimental lace. Officer's coats were dyed scarlet made from cochineal. The buttons were similar in size and shape to those on the private soldier's uniforms, but made of brass, gold, or silver.

The waistcoats and breeches were made of wool or silk, and could be scarlet in color, white, or the color of the regimental facings. Besides gaiters, officers had one or more pairs of black leather riding boots with natural colored turnovers. Officers had two or more pairs of shoes, the buckles of which were often ornate, made of steel, brass, gold, or silver. Every officer had several pairs of stockings made of finely knit linen, cotton, or silk. Officers of provincial regiments wore uniforms identical in cut as those of the regular army, but sometimes of different colors:

"Every Officer of the Virginia Regiment is as soon as possible, to provide himself with an uniform Dress, which is to be of fine Broad Cloth: the Coat Blue, faced and cuffed with Scarlet and Trimmed with Silver: The Waistcoat Scarlet, with a plain Silver Lace (if to be had) the Breeches to be Blue; and every one to provide himself with a Silver-laced Hat, of a fashionable size".[470]

Officers of highland regiments could wear plaids, kilts, or breeches, and either hose, leggings, or boots. In 1759, Captain Stewart of the 42ⁿᵈ Regiment recorded:

"When the Regt is under arms the officers are always to be in boots & knee briches".[471]

Not only was the quality of the officers clothing superior to that of the rank and file, but they also owned a great deal more of it. Included in the effects of the deceased Lieutenant Emanuel Hess in 1759 were 17 worked ruffled shirts, 19 pairs of cotton stockings, 3 pairs of white silk stockings, 2 regimental coats, and 2 pairs of breeches.[472]

Besides regiment coats, officers sometimes had simple laceless frock coats. A general order for the 42nd Regiment in January of 1760 read:

"The officers of both battalions (it is agreed) are to be uniform in their regimental frocks, which are to be made with a lapel, a collar and a slash cuff, the buttons to be the same as those sent from England for their new lacd Regimentalls".[473]

No badges or symbols, such as chevrons or stars, were worn on officer's uniforms to differentiate the various commissioned ranks. The uniform of an ensign or general could be virtually the same. Several universal items were worn by officers of all ranks. A gold or silver aiguilette (shoulder knot) was worn hanging from the right shoulder, a long crimson sash of finger woven silk was worn over the right shoulder or around the waist, and a crescent shaped "gorget" made of gilded brass or silver was worn on a ribbon around the neck. Gorgets were engraved with the king's arms or regimental devices.

Gorget, c. 1750-1760
Length: 5.49"
Width: 4.89"
*Collection of the
Fort Ticonderoga Museum*

Officer's silk sash, c. 1755-1800
Courtesy Col. J. Craig Nannos

Officers had the luxury to embellish their uniforms according to their own taste, but not all officers were inclined towards flashy uniforms with gold lace and braid. Some officers, like Robert Dinwiddie, had simpler tastes:

"...as his M'y is pleased to make me a military Officer, please send for Scott, my Taylor, to make me a proper Suit of Regimentals...I do not much like Gayety in Dress, but I conceive this necessary. I do not much care for Lace on the Coat, but a neat Embroider'd Buttonhole...a good lac'd hatt and two p'r stock'gs, one of silk, the other of fine thread".[474]

Those officers belonging to orders of chivalry or political clubs and organizations were allowed to wear their respective medals and badges, such as the badge of the Order of the Garter, Order of the Bath, Order of the Thistle, the Cumberland Society, and the Blue and Orange Society.[475]

Officers had to furnish themselves with the necessities needed to live and perform their duties, which may have included one or more horses, saddles, pistol holsters, a marquee tent with poles, a folding field bed, mattress, pillows, sheets, blankets, combs, razors, writing implements, and paper.

Captain's and sub-altern's marquee tents were made of linen canvas, measuring 14 feet long, 10 feet 6 inches wide, and 8 feet tall, with 4 foot half walls. Lieutenant colonel's and major's tents were identical, except one foot longer.[476] To keep warm, small stoves were sometimes used, the tops of which protruded through a hole cut in the ceiling. Simple stoves could also be made of sod, as Corporal Todd explained, included *"a trench dug in their marquee about 4 foot Long & in the Center of it is a Hole made that runs under the skirt of the Cloth & is soded round for a chimney".*[477]

Badge of the Cumberland Society c. 1746-1750 *Private collection*

Lieutenant Parker Steele, 23rd Regiment Royal Welsh Fusiliers, 1764 *Private collection*

This miniature portrait shows Lieutenant Steele wearing what could be a Blue and Orange Society badge on a blue ribbon around his neck.

Gold badge of the Blue and Orange Society c. 1730-1760 *Private collection*

Wood planking was sometimes placed on the floors of the tents. In September of 1757, Captain Knox wrote:

"...They are order'd to bed their tents well with the boughs of spruce for want of straw and the officers have got boards to floor their markees".[478]

Wood was delivered to the officer's tents every two days at the rate of two cords for field officers, one half cord for captains, and three quarters of a cord for subalterns (who slept two to a tent).[479] The orderly book for General Gage's brigade at Montreal in 1762 recorded the winter and summer firing for officer's messes as follows:

*"To Lieut. Col. commanding: . . .3 Chords per week
Major: . . . . .2 Chords
Officers of each company: . . . . .1 Chord
Chaplain, Surgeon & Mate,
Adjutant & Quartermaster each: 1 Chord
Summer firing: . . . . .half of above".*[480]

As the amount of wood issued sometimes proved to be insufficient, more could sometimes be purchased when available. During the winter of 1761, the officers of the 12th Regiment regularly paid Corporal Todd and his pioneers to supply them with wood:

"Lieutt Stappleton got a fire place made in his Markey, as did the most of our Officers, & agread with me to furnish them with wood ready Cutt at a Dollar per week".[481]

Some officers brought with them a variety of luxury items such as fine china, silver dinnerware, and furniture such as tables (complete with table linens), chairs, couches, and writing desks. The expenses of Lord Loudoun's secretary John Appy included a pair of silver mounted spectacles, a gold snuff box, fur gloves, a varnished toothpick case, perfumes, and a silver coffee pot.[482] Wolfe, when serving in Scotland, sent for his favorite hunting dog, fishing poles, flies, and his personal hunting guns.[483]

Spectacles, c. 1752-1780
shown actual size
Private American collection

In times of war, or on particular campaigns where the army needed to travel light, officers were forced to make do with only a bare minimum of baggage. Such was the case during the 1758 campaign against Fort Ticonderoga when the officers were ordered to carry no more than *"...a soldier's tent, a small port-mantle, blankets, & bearskin".*[484]

In January of 1759, General Amherst made the following recommendation to General Edward Whitmore, the Governor of Louisbourg:

"The officers will find out a great conveniency in having small Horsemen's Tents, I would recommend it to the whole, for if we come to any marching in this country, the great Tents will certainly be left behind".[485]

For self defence, officers carried swords, and often one or more pistols. Swords and pistols were private purchases; thus came in a variety of shapes and styles. Some officers chose to wear smallswords like the one below when off duty, while a more rugged sword was often used when on duty. Pikes or "spontoons" were carried by lieutenants and captains, which were more a symbol of rank than for defense (see page 107).

Dutch made brass tobacco box commemorating the battle of Minden (1759)
Private collection

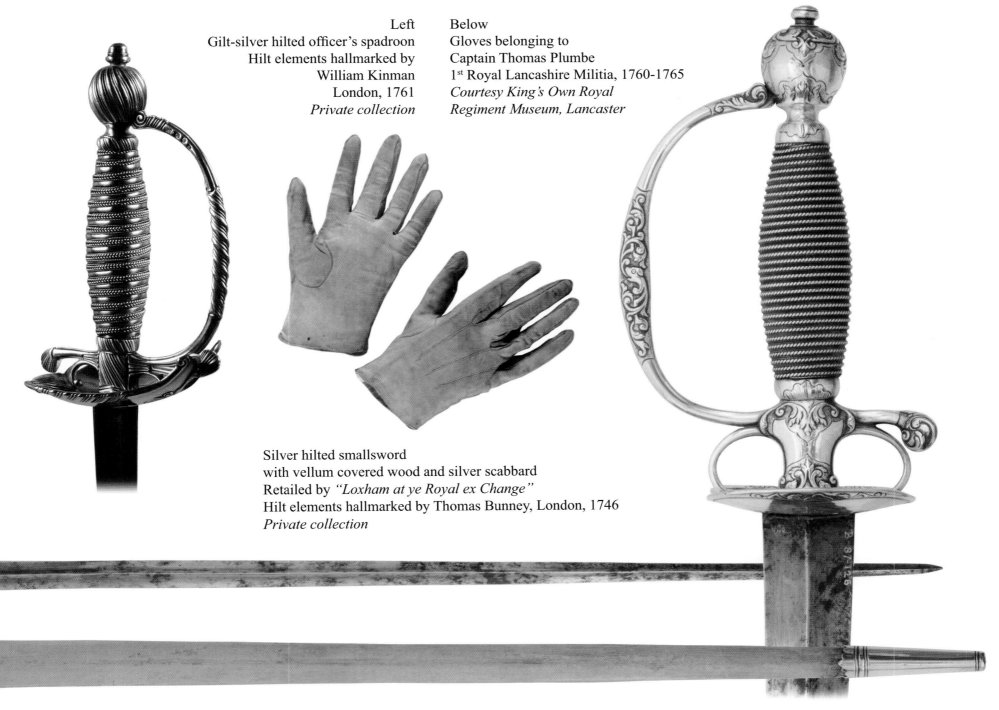

Left
Gilt-silver hilted officer's spadroon
Hilt elements hallmarked by
William Kinman
London, 1761
Private collection

Below
Gloves belonging to
Captain Thomas Plumbe
1st Royal Lancashire Militia, 1760-1765
Courtesy King's Own Royal
Regiment Museum, Lancaster

Silver hilted smallsword
with vellum covered wood and silver scabbard
Retailed by *"Loxham at ye Royal ex Change"*
Hilt elements hallmarked by Thomas Bunney, London, 1746
Private collection

"The Honble. Robert Monckton, Brigadier General; Governor
of Anapolis, Lieut. Govr. of Nova Scotia; and Colonel of his
Majesty's 17th Regt. of Foot", 1760
Library and Archives Canada. C-011220

Receipt for 20 ½ yards of silver lace and a crimson silk sash, 1755
Private collection

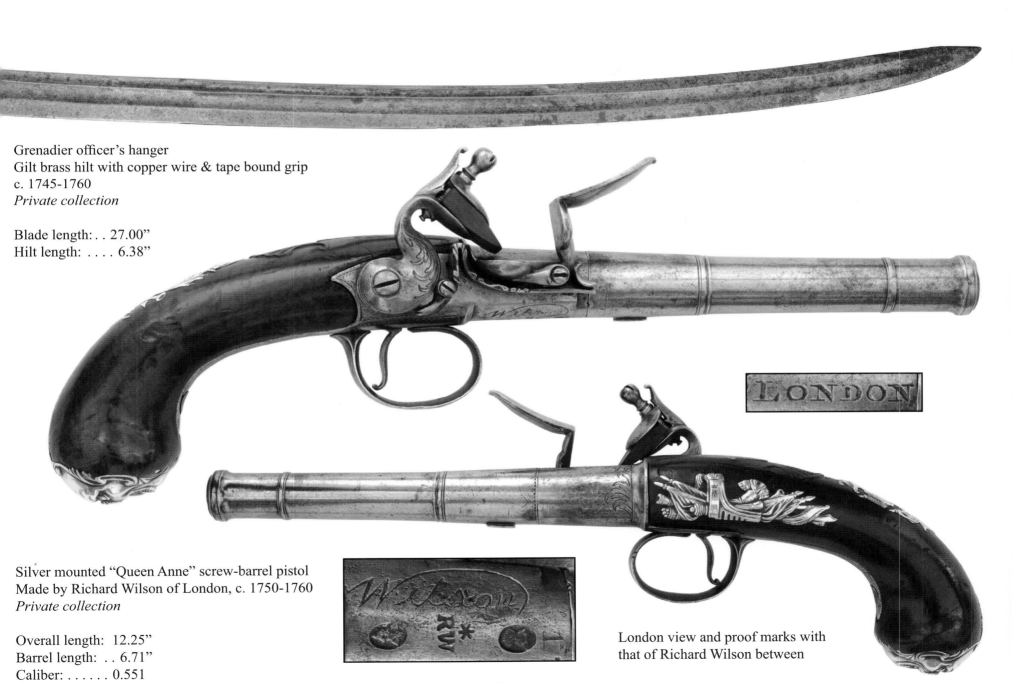

Grenadier officer's hanger
Gilt brass hilt with copper wire & tape bound grip
c. 1745-1760
Private collection

Blade length: . . 27.00"
Hilt length: . . . . 6.38"

Silver mounted "Queen Anne" screw-barrel pistol
Made by Richard Wilson of London, c. 1750-1760
Private collection

Overall length: 12.25"
Barrel length: . . 6.71"
Caliber: 0.551

London view and proof marks with
that of Richard Wilson between

Officer's fusil
By Charles Pickfatt of London, c. 1745
Private collection

Overall length: . . . . .55.19"
Barrel length: . . . . .39.75"
Caliber: 0.69

Entry pipe length: . . . .3.53"
Butt plate tang length: 4.10"
Butt plate height:. . . . .3.88"

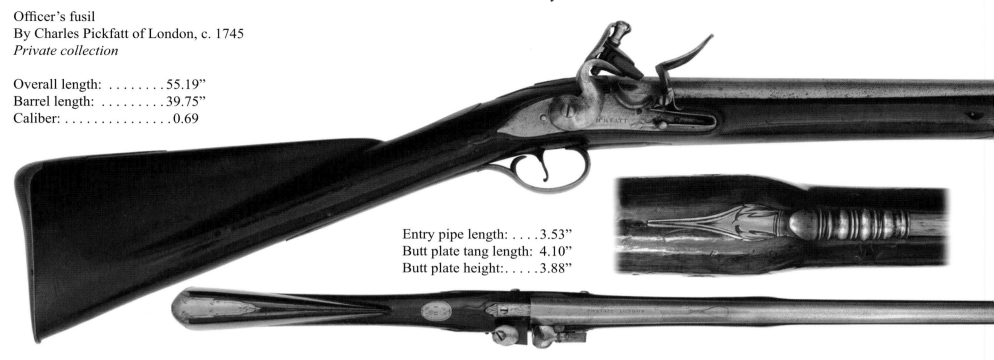

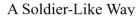

The gunmaker's name and location are engraved along the top of the breech

In America, spontoons were often left in storage, and officers instead purchased fusils:

"His Excellency (General Braddock) *likewise recommends it to all the Officers to provide them selves if possible with Fuzeis, as Espontoons will be extremely inconvenient and useless in the Woods".*[486]

"...on the 9th instant in the Evening a fuzee Belonging to Capt: Aerburcrunby Were as Supposed taken by mistake as it was Lying Near His Tent Who Ever hath it are Desired to Send it To the General, it is Marked Ransford on the Lock and Made in Dublin. A Regimental Fuzee Belonging to the 44th: Marked Barbour in the Lock and Barrel Whoever has it are Desired to Return it to Lieut: Plolony".[487]

Fusils were smoothbored firearms, often used for small game hunting in civilian life. Those intended for military use were built with bayonet lugs instead of front sights. Fusils were lighter and smaller in caliber than military muskets, sometimes with ornate carved stocks and engraved metal work. When fusils were unavailable, officers were forced to use regular issue muskets, or sometimes even captured French weapons, as Knox recorded in May of 1759:

"...The Officers of the 43rd Regiment were not all supplied with light arms; and that hitherto they had been necessitated to carry common firelocks, when detached upon duty, which were heavy and inconvenient; his excellency was pleased to order, that the regiment should be immediately provided with French fusils and other light arms from the magazine".[488]

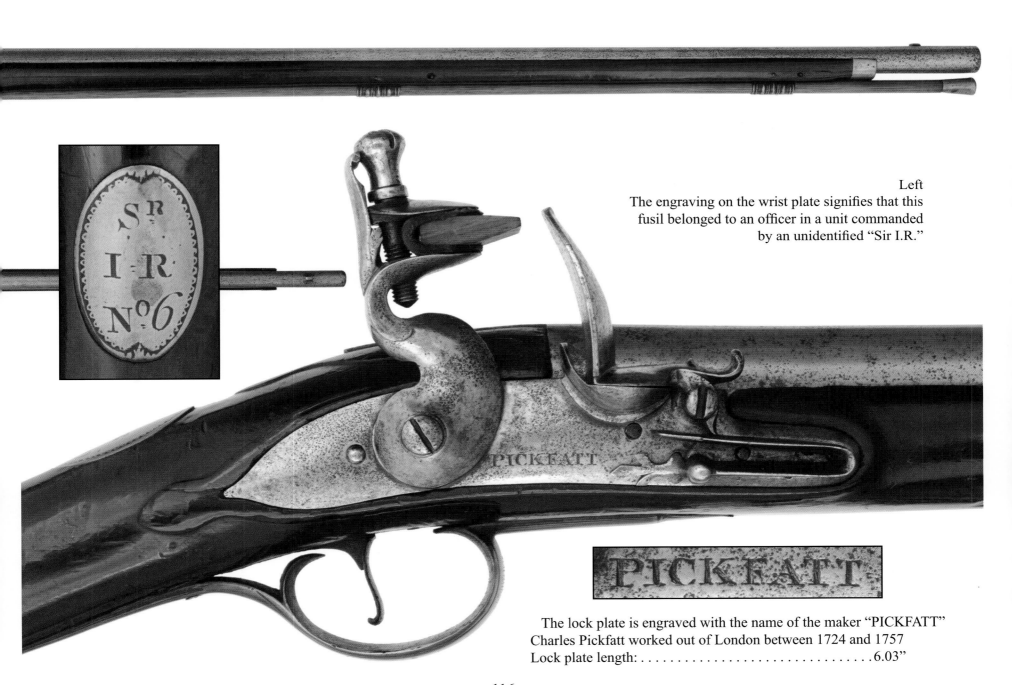

Left
The engraving on the wrist plate signifies that this fusil belonged to an officer in a unit commanded by an unidentified "Sir I.R."

The lock plate is engraved with the name of the maker "PICKFATT"
Charles Pickfatt worked out of London between 1724 and 1757
Lock plate length: . . . . .6.03"

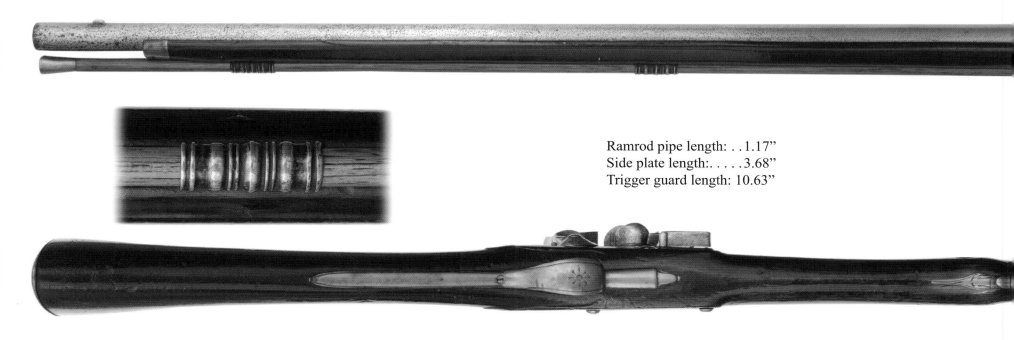

Ramrod pipe length: . . 1.17"
Side plate length: . . . . . 3.68"
Trigger guard length: 10.63"

Officers were never to actually fire their weapons unless in desperate circumstances, as Knox described:

"Officers have fusils, none of them will be so inconsiderate as to amuse themselves in firing at the enemy, by which they would inevitably neglect the much more essential part of service – the care of their platoons, and he absolutely forbids the officers firing unless on emergent occasions".[489]

Training and experience was needed for a man to become a good officer, as Bland remarked:

"A commission, it is true, qualifies a man for the pay: but it must be time and experience, and a thorough application to the service, that entitles him to the application of a soldier".[490]

Officers learned their particular duties from other experienced officers, and by reading the drill manuals and published work of specialists like General Humphrey Bland:

"Consult Bland's military discipline on that head; this will be the readiest method of learning this part of your duty which is what you will be the soonest called to perform. When off duty get a Serjt. Or corporal whom the adjutant will recommend to you, to teach you the exercise of the firelock, which I beg of you to make yourself as much master of as if you were a simple soldier".[491]

Occasionally, officers would fall in with the private soldiers to practice the manual exercise. Knox recorded in June of 1758:

"The officers for their Instruction and amusement, fall into the ranks as privates and practice all the evolutions of firing".[492]

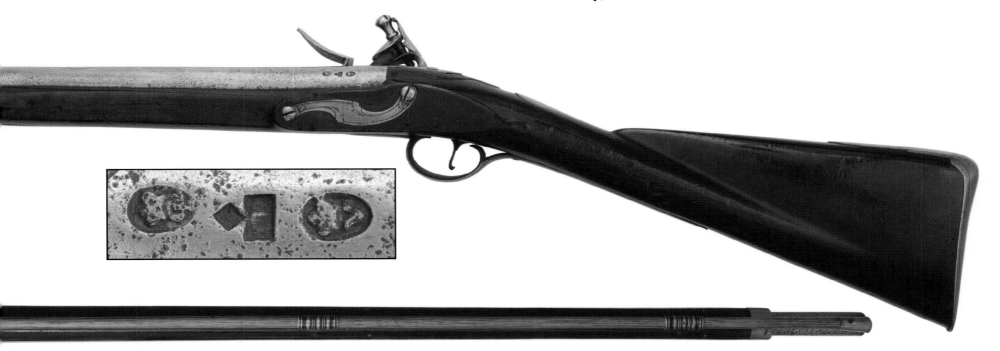

Above
London proof and view marks
with that of Charles Pickfatt between

Officers were allowed servants to aid them in dressing, cleaning, cooking, and other camp duties. Likewise, "batmen" were hired to attend to the officer's horses. The government provided an allowance for the pay and sustenance of three servants for each captain, and one to two for subalterns.[493] At times, private soldiers and musicians acted as officers' servants. In wartime, when soldiers could not be spared, local civilians or freed slaves were hired:

"As the Officers will be Allowd no baugtmen Or Servts: from the Regts they are to pitch upon baggage men in the best manner they Can from the Country people, which the Government will pay for at the rate of 3s-6d per week each man And the same allowences of provisions as the Soldiers".[494]

"The Officers may Imploy the Drummers and Fifes to wait on them, but no Soldier, Excepting Bautmen on any Pretence whatsoever".[495]

Lieutenant Colonel Samuel Bagshawe recorded the following in his account of expenditures in 1749:

"Whenever I am in Dublin, I am obliged to keep two servants on account of my horses, in the country I keep one: their wages, board and clothes upon an average is £34, 12s, 6d".[496]

Officers' servants wore their personal clothing, or if a soldier, their regimentals. Some officers, like many wealthy civilians, may have purchased liveried clothing for their servants.

In their free time, officers enjoyed the luxury of hunting, fishing, and riding. Gaming, drinking, and singing were common in the afternoon or evenings:

"...this very afternoon as we were drinking tea and singing French songs under Pitt's new tent there comes a scoundrel full gallop...and produces an order to march tomorrow morning".[497]

"The Officers, for passing away the time, made Horse Races, and agreed that no Horse should run over 11 Hands and to carry 14 Stone".[498]

When in cities, officers attended plays, musical performances, and balls, as Colonel Bagshawe recorded while in Dublin in 1742:

"To divert in the City, on Mondays and Tuesdays there are plays at two houses On Wednesday the Town has of late been entertain'd with musical performances…on Saturday is a Ball at which are generally present from six to eight hundred persons, there are besides these musical assemblies for charitable uses and others at private houses…".[499]

Popular games played by soldiers and civilians alike included billiards, bowling, whist, draughts, and commerce.[500] Mail was regularly sent and received, allowing officers to receive newspapers, clothing, books, and personal items from home.

Whereas the rank and file were issued one ration, officers received several, the number of which increased with rank at the following rates:

Brigadier General:. . . . . .12 rations per day
Colonel:. . . . . .6 rations
Lieutenant Colonel:. . . . . .5 rations
Lieutenant Colonel or
Major in command of a battalion: 6 rations
Major: . . . . .4 rations
Captain:. . . . . .3 rations
Lieutenants and Ensigns: . . . . . . .2 rations [501]

Instead of receiving the government's rations, officers could instead be paid their value in cash at the rate of four pence per ration:

"Each Capt is allowed 3 rations per day, Lieuts & Ensigns 2 Rations each, non-commissioned officers & private men one ration each. The officers who choose to have their Rations paid in money are to receive from me 4d for each ration agreeable to Lord Loudoun's orders".[502]

"If an officer chuse, they may have money in lieu of provisions from the store-keepers, at a rate of four pence per ration".[503]

The account books of officers such as Samuel Bagshawe and George Washington show that officers dined out frequently. Bagshawe wrote the following in his account book regarding an officer's diet in 1749:

"The method of an officer's diet in general is breakfast at his own lodging, dinner and supper in a tavern".[504]

Officers also dined frequently at the regimental sutlers:

"All the Sutlers to provide Dinner & Suppers for the Officers of the Corps to which they belong, they giving in their Rations & paying 6d pr day for Cooking also Paying for what Liquors they drink".[505]

Much of the officers' pay was spent simply on sustaining themselves, which sometimes left them with but a little left over, as Wolfe complained:

"I give you my word that the common demand for my horse, servants, washing, lodging, and diet, is no less than three pounds, ten shillings a week…I reckon myself to have a shilling a day for what they call pocket money".[506]

When an officer perished, his personal effects were sent home, while other items of a more military nature were sold at auction:

"The effects of some officers of the 55th who were kill'd on the 8th, to be sold by auction, in the rear of the Regt.".[507]

"The effects of Lieut – Kennedy, late of Monckton's battalion, to be sold to-morrow at 10 o'clock at ye head of said Regiment".[508]

A description of the funeral of Captain Bromley of the 44th Regiment who died in May of 1755 was as follows:

"At 10 o'clock we all attended the funeral, and the ceremony was a Captain's guard marched before the corpse, with the Captain of it in the rear, and the fire locks reversed, the drums beating the dead march. When we came near the grave, the guard formed 2 lines facing each other; rested on their arms, muzzles downwards; and leaned their faces on the butts: the Corpse was carried between them, the sword and sash on the coffin, and the officers following two and two. After the Clergyman had read the service, the guard fired 3 vollies over him and returned".[509]

Opposite
Grenadiers, 46th, 47th, and 48th Regiments of Foot, 1751
by David Morier
The Royal Collection © 2007
Her Majesty Queen Elizabeth II

46 REGIMENT

47 REGIMENT

48 REGIMENT

Wartime Alterations

No matter how prepared an army is in times of peace, it is always forced to adapt to changing environments and circumstances during wartime. A uniform suited to a European climate may be quite unsuited to the freezing winters of America or the sweltering summers of the Caribbean. General Wolfe wrote to Lord George Sackville from Halifax in 1758:

"...our clothes, our arms, our accouterments, nay even our shoes and stockings are all improper for this country".[510]

The sweeping changes that took place throughout the French & Indian War in America began with General Braddock, when on campaign against Fort Duquesne in 1755, he issued his soldiers lighter linen small clothes to combat the heat, removed their bulky cartridge pouches, waistbelts, and swords to reduce weight, replaced his NCO's cumbersome halberds with muskets, and issued rifles to the regiment's sharpshooters.[511] In 1757, Major Burd proposed dressing Pennsylvania soldiers in camouflaged clothing:

"As our Soldiers are not equal to Indians in the Woods, I think it would be a great assistance to them were they supplyed with a green shirt, a green jacket, a green blankett, and a green Cloth Capp; as the Summer is the chief time of Action, at which season of the year the woods being very thick of green leaves...".[512]

The most dramatic changes occurred in 1758 and 1759 when the thick wooded terrain of North America and the French and Indian's superior brush fighting abilities forced the British army to create a corps of light infantry. Lord Howe set the pace with his own 55th Regiment in 1758 by cutting the long tails off his men's coats and removing the lace, cropping their long hair, and cutting down their hats into short brimmed round caps. Instead of gaiters, Indian style wool leggings were issued. The musket barrels were shortened to reduce weight, and browned to reduce glare.[513] Other regiments soon followed Lord Howe's example. A deserter of the 17th Regiment in October 1758 was reported to be wearing *"...his Regimental Coat, cut short in the Skirts, and the Brim of his Hat cut very narrow...".*[514] The entry in Major John Hawks' orderly book for June 21st, 1759 states:

"In all partys it is further ordered that all Great Hats are cut so that the Brims be 2 inches and a half wide...".[515]

In 1758, the 80th Regiment of Light Armed Foot was raised in America as the first light infantry regiment on the regular establishment, with uniforms and accouterments suited for the American back woods. Likewise, in 1759, the 85th Regiment (Royal Volunteers) was raised in England, and the 90th Regiment raised in Ireland as light infantry regiments.[516]

A soldier of the 80th Regiment taken from:
"View of the Lines at Lake George, 1759"
by Thomas Davies, 1774

The 1758 Clothing Warrant describes the 80th Regiment as having short, dark brown coats, dark brown facings, black buttons, and no lace.[517] An inspection return for the 85th Regiment in March of 1760 described the uniform and accouterments as follows:

"The officers and men had swords, the officers armed with fuzees, and have cross buff belts. They wear sashes round the waist...The arms much lighter than those of the infantry. Officers and men have hangers...accoutrements new, pouch belt much narrower than which is used by the infantry, the waistbelt worn across the shoulder. The men have red coats without lapels, blue cuffs and capes with white loops lined white – double breasted short waistcoats of white cloath, breeches of the same – hats cocked in the manner of King Henry VIII with a narrow white lace, and plume of white feathers, no white or black gaiters but a black leather gaiter which comes half way up the leg".[518]

In September of 1759, one company from every regiment was turned into a "light" company, as Knox explains:

"A body of light infantry will be formed, from different corps to act as irregulars, the regiments that have been any time in America are to furnish such as have been accustomed to the woods, and are good marksmen, and those from Europe are to furnish active marchers, and men that are expert at firing ball; and all in general must be alert, spirited soldiers able to endure fatigue".[519]

"...this company will always be drawn up on the left of the battalion, and will consist of a tenth of the corps".[520]

Knox left us the following detailed description of the light infantry's clothing, as ordered by the Commander-in-Chief General Amherst:

"The sleeves of the coat are put on the waistcoat and instead of coat sleeves, he has two wings like the Grenadiers but fuller, and a round slope reaching about half-way down his arm, which makes his coat of no incumberance to him, but can be slipt off with pleasure, he has no lace, but the lapels remain: besides the usual pockets he has two, not quite so high as his breast, made of leather, for ball and flints, and a flap of red cloth on the inside, which secures the ball from rolling out if he should fall. His knapsack is carried very high between his shoulders and is fastened with a strap of web over his shoulder, as the Indian carries their pack".[521]

Light infantrymen were not issued their clothing made in this fashion, but were issued standard regimental uniforms, which were then altered by the regimental tailors to conform to General Amherst' orders:

"The men are to keep their carbines, powder boxes and are to wear their new clothing but not to cut it into the Light Infantry dress until further orders".[522]

To augment their supply of cartridges, light infantrymen were supplied with powder horns, which could hold upwards of one pound of gunpowder:

"As all the corps are now provided with powder horns, it is the Generals orders that none of the men load with cartridges upon their regimental parades, but from these powder horns...".[523]

To ensure that the proper proportion of ball and powder were issued, cartridges were simply broken open, the powder poured into the powder horn, and the ball pocketed, or carried in a leather shot pouch.[524] It is possible that the cartridge paper was also pocketed, as loading the musket required wadding *"above and below the ball to keep both powder and ball firm in their pieces"*, as Knox explained.[525] Tomahawks with leather covers were issued to the light infantrymen in lieu of swords, which were worn in the sword slot of their waistbelt frogs.

Carbines were issued to the light infantry instead of the larger Long Land pattern muskets. If not enough carbines were available, captured French muskets were sometimes shortened and issued, as General Amherst recorded in April of 1759:

"As I have cut the French Arms shorter which makes them much lighter and Handyer for the Light Infantry I shall Send you to Elizebeth Town Seventy five Firelocks which are for the three Sergeants inclusively".[526]

The shorter, smaller caliber carbines appeared to be unpopular with many soldiers, and in February of 1760, they were again issued muskets:

"The light infantry companies are now incorporated under the command of Major Dalling of the twenty-eighth regiment; and are ordered to be completed with firelocks instead of short carbines, at their own request".[527]

In extreme heat, soldiers were sometimes allowed to do duty without their regimental coats, and sometimes even without their waistcoats. An order issued to the army at Lake George in July of 1759 stated:

"The men to land in their waistcoats, go as light as possible, carry only their Blanket & Provisions".[528]

While encamped before Fort Lewis in August of 1760, Amherst wrote to Colonel Frederick Haldimand:

"The Grenadiers will Land in their Shirts, Caps on & Broad Swords flung over their Shoulders".[529]

Powder horn, 1757
Courtesy of A. Rehder

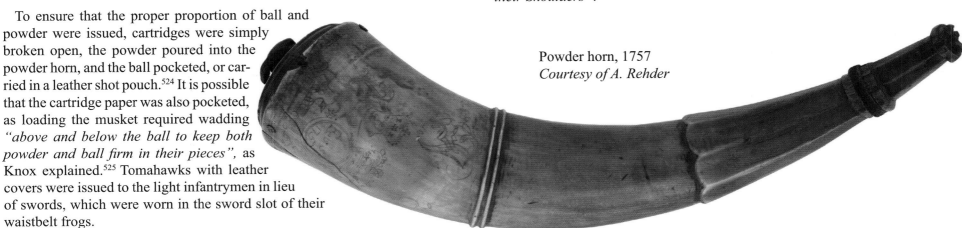

Discharge

At the onset of peace, regiments were reduced in strength, or in the case of many newly raised regiments, disbanded, and the soldiers drafted into other regiments or discharged. Those soldiers who were less fit or advanced in years were the first to be discharged. Soldiers could be discharged from the service at any time due to illness or wounds sustained in combat, while soldiers who enlisted for a specific length of time were discharged when it expired. Discharged soldiers were entitled to keep their clothing, belts, and knapsacks, which they had paid for, while their weapons and accouterments were returned to storage:

"Each non Commissioned Officers, and private men discharged be permitted to carry away with them their Cloathes, Belts, and knapsacks, which they now wear".[530]

The government paid for the transportation of discharged soldiers back to their country of origin, and once arrived, gave each soldier fourteen days subsistence money for food and lodging on their journey home.[531] Occasionally, discharged soldiers in America were allowed to stay and settle there, and, as in the case of 42nd Regiment when it was reduced in 1763, were sometimes even offered land:

"All reduced Officers, Non Comissioned officers, & Private men reduced have the offer of having land granted to them in America".[532]

Soldiers on the English establishment could apply for a pension through Chelsea Hospital in London, and those on the Irish establishment, the Kilmainham hospital in Dublin.[533] The Royal hospitals paid pensions to discharged soldiers, called "out-pensioners", and housed and fed those with infirmities or advanced in years, called "in-pensioners". Colonel Bouquet wrote to General Napier in July of 1757:

"I have by Lord Loudoun's express command inspected here the three independent Companys, and out of the 69 men who were here, the rest being in the forts, I found 17 totally unfit for service, 6 of them being very old Soldiers are recommended for Chelsea's Hospital".[534]

A notice in the Ipswich Journal on March 31st, 1759 read:

"Several Highlanders have arrived home from America to be admitted to Chelsea Hospital, four have been scalped and left for dead".[535]

Between 1761 and 1762, the Chelsea Hospital maintained as in-pensioners: 36 officers, 78 non-commissioned officers, and 336 privates.[536] Every soldier was paid according to his rank at the rate of six pence a day for officers, two shillings a week for sergeants, ten pence a week for corporals, and seven to eight pence a week for privates.[537] Every private and non-commissioned officer received each day one pound of meat, one pound of bread, one quarter pound of cheese, two pints of beer, and a penny for tobacco, while officers received slightly more.[538] Part of the money that paid for the upkeep of the pensioners and hospitals was taken from stoppages of one day's pay per year from all officers and soldiers on active duty, a percentage taken from every pound issued to the paymasters, and a percentages taken from every officer's commission sold.

Evolution, 1763-1768

After the Seven Years War, military uniforms began to evolve rapidly. These early years of evolutions were caused, in part, from wartime experience and changing civilian fashions. Full gaiters were replaced with half-gaiters sporting leather tops. Eventually those were replaced with ankle length spatterdashes. White small clothes became more popular than the traditional red. The brims of cocked hats became taller, and coats and waistcoats became shorter. Buttons bearing regimental numbers and decorative borders became popular, and were officially mandated for all regiments in 1767.[539] Like the uniforms, the weapons and accouterments also evolved. Musket barrels were shortened, and the brasswork changed shape. Knapsacks went from leather to linen and given an additional shoulder strap. As swords rarely left storage, waistbelts were no longer made to accommodate them. Some regiments switched to shoulder mounted bayonet carriages rather than waistbelts. These alterations often materialized among the officers first, who then imposed them on their soldiers. Many changes occurred without official approval, but the Clothing Board gave regimental commanders some liberties in this area. As King George III and the Clothing Board worked on new clothing regulations, they considered many of these popular alterations. The end result was the Royal Clothing Warrant of 1768.

Numbered buttons
c. 1767-1780
Photographed by the author
with permission from
The Colonial Williamsburg Foundation

Opposite:
Grenadiers, 49th Regiment of Foot,
Fifer and Drummer, Foot Guards,
by David Morier, 1751
*The Royal Collection © 2007
Her Majesty Queen Elizabeth II*

49
REGIMENT

Notes

1. Fortescue, J.W., *History of the British Army,* Vol. II. (London: Macmillan, 1910-1930), p. 30-48.

2. Guy, A.J., *Oeconomy and discipline, officership and administration in the British army, 1714-63.* (Manchester: Manchester University Press, 1985), p. 9-10. See also Houlding, J.A. *Fit For Service, The Training of the British Army, 1715 –1795.* (Oxford: Oxford University Press, 1981), p. 9-11.

3. July 15th, 1757. Bouquet, Henry, *Papers of Col. Henry Bouquet,* Series 21631 & 21632. (Harrisburg: Pennsylvania historical commission, 1940), p. 33. See also Cuthbertson, Bennet, *A system for the complete interior management and oeconomy of a battalion of infantry.* (Dublin: 1768), Chapter XI, Article VI.

4. See Thomas Potter Esq. to William Pitt, September 11th, 1757. Pitt, William, Earl of Chatham, *Correspondence of William Pitt, Earl of Chatham,* Vol. I. (London: 1838), p. 258-259.

5. Capt. John Schlosser to Col. Henry Bouquet. Philadelphia, April 26th, 1764. *Bouquet papers,* Series 21650, Part I. p.113.

6. The exact origin of the term "Brown Bess" is unknown. It is found in print as early as 1771 in the Connecticut Courant, April 2-9, 1771, #328.

7. Darling, Anthony D., *Red Coat and Brown Bess.* Historical Arms Series No. 12. (New York: Museum Restoration Service, 1971), p. 15-19.

8. *Ibid.,* p. 36.

9. Houlding, p. 147

10. Hawley, General, *"Chaos, or a rude collection of crude conceptions without connection, useful ingredients for a noble composition".* December 1726. Found in the Journal of the Society for Army Historical Research (JSAHR), Vol. XXVI, No. 107, Rev. Percy Sumner, ed. (1948), p. 91-94.

11. *Ibid.*

12. *Exercise for the Foot, with the differences to be observed in the Dragoon Exercise 1757. By Order Of H.R.H. Prince William Augustus Duke of Cumberland.* Reprinted as Historical Arms Series, No. 42. (Bloomfield, Ont: Museum Restoration Service, 2004), p. 21.

13. Stewart, Richard W., *The English Ordnance Office, A Case Study in Bureaucracy, 1585-1625.* (Rochester, Royal Historical Society, Boydell Press: 1996), p. 9.

14. *Darling,* p. 15.

15. Blackmoore, Howard L., *British Military Firearms 1650-1850.* (Mechanicsburg, PA.: Stackpole Books, 1994).

16. See Bailey, De Witt, *British Military Small Arms in North America, 1755-1783.* (The Bulletin of the American Society of Arms Collectors, 1994), p. 71/3-71/7.

17. See Peter Schuyler to William Shirley. Shirley, William, & Charles Henry Lincoln, *Correspondence of William Shirley, governor of Massachusetts and military commander in America, 1731-1760.* (New York: Macmillan Co., 1912), p. 276-277.

18. February 4th, 1760. Stewart, Captain James. *Order Book of the Royal Highland Regiment 1759-1761.* Wm. B. Wilson, ed. (Perth: Black Watch Museum, 1947).

The annual expenses of a soldier in the 68th Regiment in 1758 included funds for *"worms, keys, pickers, and brushes".* A Soldier's Journal, containing a particular description of the several descents on the coast of France last war : with an entertaining account of the islands of Guadaloupe, Dominique, &c. and also of the isles of Wight and Jersey : to which are annexed, Observations on the present state of the army of Great Britain. (London: 1770).

19. September 20th, 1761. *Stewart's.*

20. Robert Stewart to George Washington, March 12th, 1761. Hamilton, Stanislaus, M, ed. *Letters to Washington and Accompanying Papers.* The Society of the Colonial Dames of American. (Cambridge: 1898-1902). Library of Congress online: http://memory.loc.gov/ammem/gwhtml/gwhome.html.

Colonel Henry Bouquet's list of stores wanted at Carlisle, June 3rd 1758 included *"100 Bear Skins to make Covers to the Locks of the Arms".* Bouquet, Henry, *The Papers of Henry Bouquet,* Vol. II, The Forbes Expedition. K.S. Stevens, ed. (Harrisburg: Pennsylvania Historical Commission, 1951), p. 21.

21. June 28th, 1758. Amherst, Jeffery, *Journal of Jeffery Amherst.* J. Clarence Webster, ed. (Toronto: Ryerson Press, 1931), p. 55.

22. July 2nd, 1755. Robert Orme's Journal. Found in: *The history of an expedition against Fort Du Quesne, in 1755, under Major-General Edward Braddock.* Winthrop, Sargent, ed. (Philadelphia: Historical Society of Pennsylvania, 1855), p. 346.

23. March 13th, 1759. *Stewart's.*

See also Cuthbertson, Chapter XIII, Article X: *"The flints should always be screwed in firm, between a thin piece of lead, it having a more certain hold, than leather, or any other contrivance: besides a good one in his piece, a soldier ought to have another in his pouch. and a small bit of wood, shaped like a flint to exercise, in practising the firing motions, as the frequent striking up the hammers, must unavoidably break and spoil the flints, without answering any useful end".*

24. July 2nd, 1755. *Robert Orme's Journal,* p. 346.

25. Todd, William, *The Journal of Corporal Todd 1745-1762.* Andrew Cormack, Alan Jones, ed. Publications of the Army Records Society, Vol. 18. (2001), p. 157.

26. *Houlding,* p. 140.

27. *Ibid.,* p. 142.

28. A Proportion of Brass Ordnance, Howitzers and Stores for the Intended Expedition to North America by Order of the Board Dated the 12th October, 1754. Pargellis, Stanley M, ed. *Military Affairs in North America 1748-65: Selected Documents from the Cumberland Papers in Windsor Castle.* (Hamden, Connecticut: Archon Books, 1969), p. 479-487.

29. Lake George Camp, June 30th, 1758. *The Moneypenny Orderly Book,* The Bulletin of the Fort Ticonderoga Museum, Vol. XII, No. 5-6, Vol. XIII, No. 1.

30. Halifax. July 21st, 1757. *Lord Loudoun Papers, General Orders, May to September, 1757.* (Huntington Library, San Marino, CA.)

31. New York, March 21st, 1759. *Stewart's.*

32. Col. Henry Bouquet to Capt. William Grant, Fort Pitt, January 19th, 1764. *Bouquet Papers,* Series 21653.

33. March, 1755. Braddock, Edward, *Major General Edward Braddock's Orderly Books, from February 26 to June 17, 1755, From the Originals, in the Congressional Library.* (Cumberland, MD: 1878), p. VIII.

34. Townshend, Charles Vere Ferrers, Sir, *The military life of Field-Marshal George first Marquess Townshend, 1724-1807, who took part in the battles of Dettingen 1743, Fontenoy 1745, Culloden 1746, Laffeldt 1747, & in the capture of Quebec 1759.* (London: J. Murray, 1901), p. 140.

35. Wolfe to Captain Rickson, Exeter, March 7th, 1755. Beckles, Willson, *The Life and Letters of James Wolfe (Wolfe Letters).* (London: W. Heinemann, 1909), p. 154.

36. *A Soldier's Journal.*

37. Lake George Camp, July 28th, 1758. *Moneypenny's Orderly Book.*

38. Lieutenant-Colonel Edward Windus to Colonel Samuel Bagshawe, Cork, September 1st, 1760. *Colonel Bagshawe and the Army of George II, 1731-1762.* Guy, A. J. ed. (Manchester: Manchester University Press, 1985), p. 226.

39. *"We shoot obliquely, and in different situations of ground, from heights downwards and contrary wise".* Wolfe to Captain Rickson, Exeter, March 7th, 1755. *Wolfe letters*, p. 154.

40. July 24th, 1757. Knox, John. *An historical journal of the campaigns in North America for the years 1757, 1758, 1759, and 1760,* Vol. I. (Freeport, NY: Books for Libraries Press, 1970), p. 38.

41. Wolfe to Captain Rickson, Exeter, March 7th, 1755. *Wolfe Letters*, p. 154.

42. June 27th, 1760. Hawks, John, *Orderly book and journal of Major John Hawks on the Ticonderoga-Crown Point campaign, under General Jeffrey Amherst, 1759-1760.* (New York: Society of Colonial Wars in the State of New York, 1911), p. 78.

43. April 4th, 1759. *Stewart's.*

44. 1760. *Knox*, Vol. II, p. 535.

45. April, 1759. *Knox*, Vol. I, p. 301.

46. Col. Henry Bouquet to Capt. Lewis Ourry, Fort Pitt, September 26th, 1764. *Bouquet Papers*, Series 21653, p. 321.

47. *Houlding*, p. 143-144.

48. West, Jenny, *Gunpowder, Government, and War in the mid-18th century.* (Rochester: Boydell Press, 1991), p. 68-69.

49. *Ibid.*, p. 7.

50. *Ibid.*, p. 28.

51. Fort Edward, July 5th, 1757. Lyman, Phineas, *General orders of 1757: issued by the Earl of Loudoun and Phineas Lyman in the campaign against the French.* (New York: Dodd, Mead, 1899), p. 39.

52. Fort Edward Camp, June 13th, 1758. *Moneypenny's Orderly Book.*

53. Fort Edward, July 7th, 1757. *Loudoun*, p. 40.

54. Gridley, Luke, *Luke Gridley's Diary of 1757 while in the service in the French and Indian War.* (Connecticut: Acorn Club of Connecticut publications, 1907), p. 28.

See also *Loudoun*, p. 8, for May 18th, 1757: *"...And That an Exact Return Be Made Every Monday Morning to See whether they Have their Number of Cartridges & those that are Deficient May Expect to be delt with as Embezzlers of ye Kings Stores Besides Paying three Pence Sterling for each Charge Expended..."*.

55. Ft. Edward, July 28th, 1757. *Loudoun*, p. 58.

56. Winchester, April 12th, 1756. *The Writings of Washington from the Original Manuscript Sources, 1745-1799.* Fitzpatrick, John C. ed. (Washington: U. S. Govt. print. off. 1931-44).

57. Simes, Thomas. *The Military Guide for Young Officers.* (London: 1776), p. 377.

58. Camp at Neaoure Bay. August. 12th, 1760. Hervey, William, *Journals of Hon. William Hervey, in North America and Europe, From 1755-1814; with Order Books at Montreal 1760-1763. With Memoir and Notes.* (Bury St. Edmund's: Paul & Mathew, 1906), p. 108.

59. Advocate General's letter book, May 2nd, 1754. *JSAHR*, Vol. XXIII. No. 94. Rev. Percy Sumner ed. (1945), p. 82-83.

60. May 22nd, 1761. Order book of the 12th foot in Germany, 1761. *JSAHR*, Vol. XXVII, No. 112. Rev. Percy Sumner, ed. (1949), p. 153-154.

61. *JSAHR*, Vol. XXIII, No. 94. (1945), p. 82-83.

62. June 23rd, 1761. *Todd*, p. 153.

63. Washington to Virginia Regiment Officers, July 29th, 1757. *Washington Manuscripts.*

64. *Cuthbertson*, Chapter XIII, article XXVII.

65. Royal American Battalion Disbursements, Halifax, July 1st, 1759. *Bouquet Papers*, Series 21654, p. 176.

66. Hawley, *Chaos*, p. 91-94.

67. *Ibid.*

68. *Guy*, p. 147.

69. Field Officer to William Shirley. *Shirley*, Vol. II, p. 276. See also Peter Schuyler to William Shirley, p. 277.

70. *JSAHR*, Vol. XXIII. No. 94. (1945), p. 82-83.

71. Bailey, DeWitt, *Pattern Dates for British Ordnance Small Arms, 1718-1783.* (Gettysburg: Thomas Publications, 1997).

72. *Guy*, p. 127.

73. Whitworth, Rex, *William Augustus, Duke of Cumberland, A Life.* (London: 1992). p. 135. See also Chartrand, Renè, *British Army Deserter and Related Descriptions of Clothing, 1754.* found in the Journal of The Company of Military Historians (JCMH), Vol. XXXV, No. 1. (Washington: 1983), p. 12.

74. *1751 Royal Clothing Warrant.* War Office (WO) 26/21, p. 502-514. National Archives, Kew.

75. *1758 Clothing Warrant.* WO, 30/13A, p. 6-8. National Archives, Kew.

76. *Guy*, p. 149.

77. Crump, W. B., Joseph Rogerson, Benjamin Gott. *Leeds Woollen Industry 1780 – 1868.* (Leeds: Thoresby Society, 1931), p. 288.

78. *Ibid.*, p. 287.

79. Tann, Jennifer, *Gloucestershire Woollen Mills : Industrial Archaeology.* (Newton Abbot, Devon: David & Charles, 1967).

80. Wolfe to his mother, Stroud, November, 1756. *Wolfe Letters*, p. 305-306.

81. Chenciner, Robert, *Madder Red, A history of luxury and trade*. (Richmond: Curzon, 2000).

82. See Edwards, E.H. *Making the Redcoat, British Army Uniform Manufacture*. Military Illustrated Magazine, #81, p. 15-16.

83. *Cuthbertson*, Chapter XII, Article VIII.

84. A description of the clothing alterations of the 13th Regiment dated January 24th, 1767 reads: *"...yellow fall down collar, in place of a common stand-up one"*. War Office (WO), 30-13a, p. 22.

85. 1758 Clothing Warrant.

86. George Washington to John Campbell, Earl of Loudoun, March, 1757. *Washington Manuscripts*.

87. *Chartrand*, p. 12.

88. *Cuthbertson*, Chapter XII, Article XIII.

89. Lieut. Alexander Baillie to Col. Henry Bouquet, August 28th, 1762. Return of the weight of the Clothing, Arms, Accouterments, Ammunition, Provisions, Necessary's & Ca of a Grenadier upon a march. *Bouquet Papers*, Series 21648, Part 2, p. 77-78.

90. June, 1755. *Orme's Journal*. Sargent, p. 298.

91. December 12th, 1758. *Knox*, Vol. I. p. 285.

92. *Cuthbertson*, Chapter XII, Article XXXIX.

93. Major Jas. Dalrymple's Orders, 1st Battalion, 1st Regiment, Dublin, August 27th, 1762. *JSAHR*, Vol. XXII. No. 91. (1944), p. 304.

94. Cork, October 3rd, 1760. *Bagshawe*, p. 228.

95. See Dominic Serres painting: *The Capture of Havana, 1762: the English Battery Before Morro Castle*. The National Maritime Museum, London, BHC0410.

96. February 21st, 1759. *Stewart's*.

97. *Wolfe Letters*, p. 99.

98. *Cuthbertson*, Chapter XII, Article XXXVI.

99. *Chartrand*, p. 12.

100. *Cuthbertson*, Chapter XIV, Article VIII.

101. Lt. Col. James Murray to Jeffrey Amherst, 1757. Houlding, J. A., *The 15th Foot in 1757*. *JSAHR*, Vol. LXIV, No. 257. (1986), p. 56-57.

102. Hawley, *Chaos*.

103. *Cuthbertson*, Chapter XII, Article XXXVIII.

104. *Ibid*. See also Washington to Robert Dinwiddie, September 11th, 1755. *"...I think it would be advisable for your Honour to send to Philadelphia for Shoes, white-yarn Stockings, Blankets, Kettles..."*. Washington Manuscripts.

105. *Cuthbertson*, Chapter XII, Article XLII.

106. *Guy*, p. 151.

107. Invoice: Clothing for the 55th Regiment, Philadelphia, July 13th, 1764. *Bouquet Papers*, Series 21654, p. 140.

108. *An act for punishing Mutiny and Desertion; and for the better Payment of the Army and their Quarters*. (London: 1758), p. 159.

109. Part of these stoppages went towards the upkeep of the Royal hospitals, and towards the officer's widow's pension fund.

110. September 21st - 30th, 1758. *Todd*, p. 104.

111. Darlington, Mary C., *Fort Pitt and Letters from the Frontier*. (Pittsburgh: J.R. Weldin & Co., 1892), p. 187.

112. *"A Return of the recruits rais'd by Capt'n Benj'n Noxon, 1758"*. Pennsylvania Archives, Second Series, Vol. II. (Harrisburg: J. Severns & Co., 1876), p. 566-568.

113. Col. Henry Bouquet to General Jeffery Amherst, Fort Pitt, December 20th, 1760. *Bouquet Papers*, Series 21634, p. 29.

114. June 4th, 1761. *Todd*, p. 142.

115. Royal American Battalion Disbursement, Halifax, July 1st, 1759. *Bouquet Papers*, Series 21654, p. 29-30.

116. *Todd*, p. 141.

117. June 2nd, 1761. *Ibid*.

118. June 6th, 1761. *Ibid*., p. 142.

119. May 13th, 1761. *Stewart's*.

120. June 3rd, 1761. *Todd*, p. 141.

121. June 2nd, 1761. *Ibid*.

122. June 11th, 1760. *Stewart's*.

123. May 13th, 1761. *Ibid*.

124. November 5th, 1759. *Stewart's*.

125. General Orders issued at Fort Edward in January, 1760. *Ibid*.

126. *Simes*, p. 247.

127. January 2nd, 1760. *Stewart's*.

128. *Cuthbertson*, Chapter XII, Article XII.

129. January 2nd. *Stewart's*.

130. *Order book of the 12th Foot in Germany, 1761*. JSAHR, Vol. XXVII, No. 112. Rev. Percy Sumner, ed. (1949), p. 153-154.

131. *Cuthbertson*, Chapter XII, Article XIV.

132. May 12th, 1761. *Order book of the 12th Foot in Germany,*, p. 153-154.

133. *Ibid*.

134. *"They (the tailors) are Obliged to make us a foraging Cap of the pieces, Every man to have one, all to be alike"*. June 4th 1761. *Todd*, p. 142.

135. *Cuthbertson*, Chapter XII, Article XIV.

136. June 3rd, 1761. *Todd*, p. 141.

137. October 15th, 1761. *Stewart's*.

138. June 4th, 1761. *Todd*, p. 141-142.

139. Findlay, J.T., *Wolfe in Scotland in the '45 and from 1749 to 1753*. (London: Longmans, Green and co., 1928), p. 160.

Shell button, c. 1754
shown actual size
Jumonville, Braddock Road Preservation Association

140. *"The General desires that we give each recruit a jacket conforming to what you have both decided upon. But as I do not know if you have already bought or ordered the cloth buttons, linen cloth, and thread for these jackets..."*. Capt. John Schlosser to Col. Henry Bouquet, Lancaster, April 6th, 1760. *Bouquet Papers*, Series 21645, p. 66-67.

141. Bland, Humphery, *A treatise of military discipline: in which is laid down and explained the duty of the officer and soldier, through the several branches of the service*, 8th Edition. (London: 1759), p. 225.

142. *The Cadet, A Military Treatise*, 2nd Edition, anon. (London: 1762), p.109.

143. June 26th, 1759. *Hawks*, p. 24.

144. *A Soldier's Journal*.

145. August 16th, 1758. *Todd*, p.83.

146. July 27th, 1760. *Stewart's*.

147. George Washington to John Campbell, Earl of Loudoun, March 1757. *Washington Manuscripts*.

148. Carlisle, June 3rd, 1758. *Bouquet Papers, Vol. II. The Forbes Expedition*, p. 18.

149. December 24th, 1761. *Todd*, p. 255.

150. *A return of Capt'n John Blackwood's Company of the Pennsylvania Regiment, May ye 22d, 1758. Pennsylvania Archives*, p. 569.

151. Fort Cumberland, June 23rd 1759. Eddy, Jonathan, *Fragment and orderly book by Capt. Jonathan Eddy, 1755-1759*. Clara A. Avery, ed. (Boston: T.O. Metcalf Co., 1927), p. 46.

152. Grant, Anne MacVicar, *Memoirs of an American lady: with sketches of manners and scenery in America*, Vol. II. (New York: G. Appleton, 1846), p. 22.

153. May 1st, 1761. *Order book of the 12th foot in Germany, 1761*, p. 153-154.

154. Cork, October 3rd, 1760. *Bagshawe*, p. 228.

See also *Washington Manuscripts*: General Orders, July 6th, 1756: *"All non-commissioned Officers and Soldiers are expressly ordered to wear their hair; which it is expected the Officers will observe; and see that they dress their hair, and appear as soldier-like as possible"*.

and *Cuthbertson*, Chapter XIV, Article XI: *"As nothing promotes the growth of hair, more than frequent combing, the Soldiers should be enjoined to accustom themselves to do so, both morning and night"*.

155. *Cuthbertson*, Chapter XIV, Article XI.

156. September 20th, 1761. *Stewart's*.

157. March 25th, 1758. *Wolfe in Scotland*, p. 143.

158. *Bland*, 8th Edition, p. 177.

159. *"Lieut Barlow, Quartermaster Serjeant Cole & the Camp Collour Men belonging our Brigade to Mark out the ground for our Encampment ready against tomorrow that we get their"*. June 17th 1761. *Todd*, p. 149.

160. *A Soldier's Journal*.

161. July 16th, 1760. *Stewart's*.

162. *A Soldier's Journal*.

163. *Ibid*.

164. *A Soldier's Journal*.

165. *Gridley*, p. 42.

166. Royal American Battalion Disbursements, Halifax, July 1st, 1759. *Bouquet Papers*, Series 21654, p. 176.

167. Fort Edward, June 28th, 1757. *Loudoun*, p. 32.

168. *"All our Camp Equipage was serv'd out, the tents Number'd & the men tented 5 Men too Each tent by the Roll"*. April 27th, 1756. *Todd*, p. 14.

See also *Cuthbertson*, Chapter IX, Article XXIII: *"all the Tents of a Regiment should, before the opening of the Campaign, be distinctly marked, with the number of the Regiment, Company and Tent : this exactness, exclusive of any other consideration, will prevent considerable trouble, by never having the Tents changed or intermixed with those of other Corps"*.

169. Capt. John Schlosser to Col. Henry Bouquet, Niagara, July 28th, 1760. *Bouquet Papers*, Series 21645, p. 126.

170. Montreal April 20th, 1761. *Stewart's*.

171. Half Way Brook February 4th, 1760. *Ibid*.

172. *Allowance of straw and firing in Ireland, 1759, judged necessary for each tent. Simes.*

173. Camp at Rees Town, June 26th, 1758. Bouquet's Order Book. *Bouquet Papers*, Vol. II. p. 660.

174. July 24th, 1759. Wolfe, James, *General Orders in Major Wolfe's Army Before Quebec*. (Toronto: Canadian House, 1967), p. 28. See also *Knox* for September 1st, 1757. p. 64.

175. July 13th, 1761. *Stewart's*.

176. *A Soldier's Journal*.

177. Bouquet to St. Clair, June 3rd, 1758. *Bouquet Papers, Vol. II, the Forbes Expedition*, p. 22.

178. Munro, Donald, M.D., *An Account of the Diseases which were most frequent in the British Military Hospitals in Germany, from January 1761 to the return of the Troops to England in March 1763*. (London: Printed for A. Millar, D. Wilson, T. Durham, 1764), p. 320.

179. *"...besides the allowance of straw, we had two blankets among us, which to prevent one man's having a greater share then another, are sewd together at the ends, and so we creep into them"*. *A Soldier's Journal*.

180. *Munro*, p. 316.

181. *A Soldier's Journal*.

182. Curtis, Edward E., *The Organization of the British Army in the American Revolution*. (London: H. Milford, Oxford University Press, 1926).

183. Pargellis, Stanley M., *Lord Loudoun in North America*. (Hamden, Connecticut: Archon Books, 1968). p. 72, 292-293.

184. *Curtis*.

185. *Lord Loudoun in North America*, p. 293.

186. *A Soldier's Journal*.

187. Camp at Fort Ontario, July 17th, 1760. *Stewart's*.

188. Orders to Lieut. Elias Meyer, Fort Pitt, August 12th, 1761. *Bouquet Papers*, Series 21653.

189. July 22nd, 1760. *Hervey*, p. 84.

190. Pouchot, Pierre, *Memoir upon the late war in North America, between the French and English, 1755-60.* Vol. I, Franklin B. Hough, ed. (Roxbury, Massachusetts: Printed for W.E. Woodward, 1866). p. 110.

191. Williams, Edward, *The Orderly Book of Colonel Henry Bouquet's Expedition against the Ohio Indians, 1764.* (Philadelphia: 1765). p. 15.

192. July 31st, 1759. *Knox*, Vol. I, p. 461.

193. Carlisle, November 15th, 1756. *Pennsylvania Archives*, Vol. III. p. 54-55.

194. August 3rd, 1759. *Knox*, Vol. II, p. 115.

195. May 21st, 1755. *Hawkett's Orderly Book*, Found in: Hamilton, Charles, *Braddock's defeat; the journal of Captain Robert Cholmley's batman, the journal of a British officer [and] Halkett's orderly book.* (Norman: University of Oklahoma Press, 1959), p. 91.

196. July 4th, 1759. *General Orders in Major Wolfe's Army Before Quebec*, p. 17.

197. *Knox*, Vol. I, p. 71-72.

198. *Ibid.*, Vol. I, p. 71.

199. *Ibid.*, Vol. I, p. 71-72.

200. *Munro*, p. 328.

201. For a list sutler's goods and prices at Reastown on August 10th, 1758, see *Bouquet*, Vol. II, p. 352-253.

202. Major-General Amherst to Major-General Wolfe, Albany, May 6th, 1759. *Amherst and the Conquest of Canada*, p. 53.

203. "We are now regaled with the root Dandelion, whose leaves make a good salad, and are equal to endives, or if boiled, eat as well as spinage", April 16th, 1758. *Knox*, Volume I, p. 159.

204. *Cuthbertson*, Chapter XII, Article XLIV.

205. Royal American Battalion Disbursements, Halifax, July 1st, 1759. *Bouquet Papers*, Series 21654, p. 176.

206. *Ibid.*

207. June, 1758. *Knox*, Volume I, p. 177.

208. *A Soldier's Journal.*

209. "This day we receiv'd our Camp Equipage from London…We have got lids too our Camp Kettles & Larger tops too our Canteens, adeal better than we had the last year…". In Quarters at Reading, May 10th, 1758. *Todd*, p. 39.

210. *Knox*, Vol. II, p. 359.

211. Royal American Battalion Disbursements, Halifax, July 1st, 1759. *Bouquet Papers*, Series 21654, p. 176.

212. A Proportion of Brass Ordnance, Howitzers and Stores for the Intended Expedition to North America by Order of the Board Dated October 12th, 1754. *Pargellis*, p. 479-487.

213. Camp at Reas Town, July 10th, 1758. Bouquet's Orderly Book. *Bouquet Papers*, Vol. II, p. 664.

214. Regulations for Provisions, April 26th 1759. *Eddy*, p. 18. See also *Gridley*, p. 32, for June 1st, 1757.

215. Halifax, July 28th, 1757. *Loudoun Papers.*

216. June 26th, 1759. *Hawks*, p. 24.

217. July 11th, 1759. *Ibid.* p. 31.

218. March, 1760. *Knox*, Vol. II, p. 355.

219. *Bland*, 8th Edition, p. 293.

220. Allowance of straw and firing in Ireland, 1759, judged necessary for each tent. *Simes.*

221. October 28th, 1761. *Todd*, p. 215.

222. *A Soldier's Journal.*

223. *Pennsylvania Archives*, Vol. III, p. 62-63.

224. *Knox*, Vol. I, p. 140.

225. Halifax, July 13th, 1757. *Lord Loudoun Papers.*

226. October 8th, 1759. *Stewart's.*

227. Captain Gavin Cochrane to Col. Henry Bouquet, Presqu Isle, August 11th, 1761. *Bouquet Papers*, Series 21647, p. 57.

228. Carlisle, November 15th, 1756. *Pennsylvania Archives*, Vol. III, p. 54-55.

229. "as provisions cannot possibly be delivered to them upon the march, each effective man who joins the army shall be paid four pence Stirling in lieu of provisions from the time he begins his march, until that time he receives provisions from the stores". Forbes, John, *Letters of General John Forbes relating to the expedition against Fort Duquesne in 1758 compiled from books in the Carnegie Library of Pittsburgh for the Allegheny County Committee, Pennsylvania Society of the Colonial Dames of America.* Stewart, Irene, ed. (Pittsburgh: Allegheny County Committee, 1927), p. 10.

230. *Knox*, Vol. I, p. 64.

231. Raestown, September 16th, 1758. *Forbes*, p. 46.

232. March 27th, 1755. *Hawkett's Orderly Book*, Hamilton, p. 65.

233. *Todd*, p. 75.

234. "…For the security of the cattle of the army, the soldiers are therefore forbid to break down any fence for firewood". June 29th, 1759. *Knox*, Vol. I, p. 384.

235. "Houses of Office to be made in the Rear of the Camp, and Wells to be dug for each Regiment, that the men may get Water as easie as possible". Camp at Ticonderoga, July 24th, 1759. Amherst, Jeffery, Wilson, & O'Callaghan, E. B., *Commissary Wilson's orderly book: expedition of the British and provincial army, under Maj. Gen. Jeffrey Amherst, against Ticonderoga and Crown Point, 1759.* (Albany: J. Munsell, 1857). See also *Munro*, p. 348.

236. October 14th, 1761. *Todd*, p. 205.

237. *Cuthbertson*, Chapter IX, Article XXIV.

238. Camp at Reas Town, June 26th, 1758. Bouquet's Orderly Book. *Bouquet Papers*, Vol. II, p. 660.

239. *Wolfe in Scotland*, p. 288.

240. *Munro*, p. 310.

241. Fort Cumberland, July 5th, 1755. *Eddy*, p. 13.

242. March 27th, 1755. *Braddock's Orderly Book*, p. V.

243. June 19th, 1758. Bouquet's Orderly Book. *Bouquet Vol. II*, p. 657.

244. July 25th, 1760. *Stewart's.*

245. October 4th, 1761. *Ibid.*

246. Fort Edward, June 20th, 1757. *Loudoun*, p. 25.

247. *Ibid.*

248. Fort Edward, August 24th, 1757. *Ibid.*, p. 73.

249. *"I am now on a detachmt. in Sussex to destroy a Gang of Smugglers who besides divers Outrages have had the Insolence to call themselves the Southern Rebells"*. Captain Samuel Bagshawe to Dr. Thomas Fletcher Eastbourne, February 7th, 1746. *Bagshawe*, p. 48.

250. June 4th, 1760. *Hawks*, p. 71.

251. Regulation of Pay for Laborers and Artificers, Albany, September 13th, 1756. *Bouquet Papers*, Series 21631 & 21632, p. 2.

252. *Wolfe in Scotland*, p. 161.

253. *Ibid.*, p. 151.

254. *Wolfe in Scotland*, p. 184.

255. *Ibid.*, p. 184.

256. *Ibid.*, p. 189.

257. Half Way Brook, January, 1760. *Stewart's.*

258. *Pargellis*, Military affairs in North America. p. 247

259. Braddock to Newcastle, Williamsburg, March 20th 1755. *Ibid.*, p. 81.

260. *"No soldier to stir out of camp, unless those who are ordered on particular duties…"*. July 9th, 1759. *Knox*, Vol. I, p. 486.

261. *Ibid.*, Vol. I, p. 137, and Vol. II, p. 19. *Bouquet Papers*, Vol. II, p. 352-353. See also Redmon, Barton J., *Grand and Petit Sutlers of the British Army during the era of the Seven Years War 1755-1765*.

262. *Seaman's Journal.* Found in *Sargent*, p. 330.

263. Foster, Henry, *The Journal of Henry Foster, of Sturbridge Massachusetts, during the French and Indian War, May 27 – October 27, 1758*, p. 4.

264. *"…soldiers are not permitted to swim in ye heat of the day, only in ye mornings and evenings"*. General Orders in Major Wolfe's Army Before Quebec, p. 27.

265. *"…Confine all Soldiers that shall Be Seen Wadeing or Swimming in the River in their Regimental Cloths…"*. Fort Edward, June 4th, 1757. *Loudoun*, p. 18.

266. Fort Edward, August 30th, 1757. *Loudoun*, p. 75.

267. Fort Edward, September 29th, 1757. *Ibid.*, p. 98.

268. Fort Cumberland. September 20th, 1759. *Eddy*, p. 88.

269. October 21st, 1758. *Todd*, p. 104.

270. *Wolfe in Scotland*, p. 160-161.

271. *Ibid.*, p. 232.

272. *Ibid.*

273. December 25th, 1759. *Knox*, Vol. II, p. 312.

Above
Spanish colonial "cob"
2 reales, Lima, Peru
c. 1701
shown actual size
Photographed by the author
with permission from
The Colonial Williamsburg Foundation

274. April 23rd, 1759. *Ibid.*, Vol. I, p. 305.

275. May 14th, 1759. *Ibid.*, Vol. I, p. 172.

276. Montreal, June 3rd, 1761. *Stewart's.*

277. March, 1755. *Orme's Journal*, *Sargent*, p. 292.

278. Camp at Ticonderoga, July 24th, 1759. *Wilson.*

279. *Amherst's Journal*, p. 289.

280. May, 1758. *Knox*, Vol. I, p. 171.

281. May, 1758. *Ibid.*, Vol. I, p. 171-172.

282. Capt. John Schlosser to Colonel Henry Bouquet, Philadelphia, March 15th, 1764. *Bouquet Papers*, Series 21650, Part I, p. 61.

283. *Halkett's Orderly Book*, *Sargent*, p. 73.

284. Forbes to Governor Denny, October 22nd, 1758. *Forbes.*

285. Wolfe, James, *Wolfe's Instructions for Young Officers.* (London: Printed for J. Millan, 1778).

286. *"Non Commissioners and private men in Garrison…make it their Daily practice to Wash and keep their Face and hands clean…"*. Fort Cumberland, January 23rd, 1759. *Eddy*, p. 46. See also *Bland*, 8th Edition, p. 225.

287. Wolfe to Lord George Sackville, Halifax, May 24th, 1758. *Wolf Letters*, p. 367.

288. *Wolfe in Scotland*, p. 298.

289. *Grant*, Vol. II. p. 23-24. See also Col. Henry Bouquet to the Earl of Loudoun, Charles Town, South Carolina, June 23rd, 1757. *"The Water is generally so bad in this Country and the heat so continual, that we have already upwards of 31 men Sick, tho' we had but five when we landed"*. *Bouquet Papers*, Series 21631 and 21632, p. 15.

290. Fort Edward, July 5th, 1757. *Loudoun*, p. 39.

291. March 16th, 1743. *To Mr. Davenport. Being letters of Major Davenport to his brother*, *JSAHR*, No. 9.

292. *Proceedings and Debates of the British Parliament Respecting North America 1754-1783*, Vol. I. Simmons, R.C., Thomas, P.D.G. eds. (Millwood, New York: Kraus, 1982), p. 25.

293. *Munro*, p. 394.

294. *Ibid.*

295. *Ibid.*, The Royal College of Physicians, London.

296. *Ibid.*, p. 400.

297. *Ibid.*, p. 359.

298. Adam Stephen to George Washington, January 18th, 1756. Washington, George, *Letters to Washington and Accompanying Papers*, published by the Society of the Colonial Dames of America. Stanislaus Murray Hamilton ed. (Boston: Houghton, Mifflin and Co., 1898).

299. *Munro*, p. 362.

300. Kirk, Robert, *The Memoirs and Adventures of Robert Kirk, Late of the Royal Highland Regiment.* (Limerick: printed by J. Ferrar, 1770).

301. *Munro*, p. 363.

302. *Munro*, p. 367.

303. *Knox*, Vol. I, p. 304.

304. *Munro*, p. 388.

305. Perry, David, *Recollections of an old soldier: the life of Captain David Perry, a soldier of the French and Revolutionary wars.* (Windsor, Vermont: Republican & Yeoman, 1822), p. 51.

306. Alexandria, Virginia, March, 1755. *Orme's Journal, Sargent*, p. 295.

307. Col. George Mercer to Col. Henry Bouquet, January 25th, 1760. *Bouquet Papers*, Series 21645, p. 19.

308. *Munro*, p. 124-244.

309. Table of diet used in the hospital in Germany 1761-1763. *Ibid.*, p. 377-378.

310. *Ibid.*, p. 315.

311. Washington to Peter Hog, January 10th, 1756. *Washington Manuscripts*.

312. *Munro*, p. 372.

313. Andrews, Frank De Witte, *Connecticut soldiers in the French and Indian war; bills, receipts and documents printed from the original manuscripts.* (Vineland, New Jersey: 1925), p. 6.

314. Washington to Paymaster Alexander Boyd, November 1st, 1755. *Washington Manuscripts*.

315. August 20th, 1759. *General Orders in Major Wolfe's Army Before Quebec*.

316. Wolfe to ?, May 9th 1759. *Wolfe Letters*, p. 426.

317. *Munro*, p. 330.

318. *"Our men take great quantities of fish over the ships sides. They are chiefly Mackerel and Polluc"*. August 12th, 1757. *Knox*, Vol. I, p. 49.

319. May 21st, 1755. *The Journal of Captain Robert Cholmley's Batman, Hamilton*, p. 15.

   See also *Stewart's* for July 17th, 1760: *"No baker of this army will be allowed to take more than one penny sterling for baking 7 pounds of flour which makes a loaf of 9 pounds weight"*.

320. July 10th, 1758. Bouquet's Orderly Book. *Bouquet Papers*, Vol. II, p. 660.

321. Lieut. Alexander Baillie to Col. Henry Bouquet, Return of the weight of the Clothing, Arms, Accouterments, Ammunition, Provisions, Necessary's & Ca of a Grenadier upon a march. August 28th, 1762. *Bouquet Papers*, Series 21648, Part 2, p. 77-78.

322. *Bland*, 8th Edition, p. 141.

323. April, 1755. *Orme's Journal, Sargent*, p. 296.

324. *Wolfe in Scotland*, p. 298.

325. Fielding, Henry, *The History of Tom Jones, a Foundling.* (London: 1749), p. 312.

326. July 17th, 1755. *Hervey*, p. 5.

327. *Bouquet Papers*, Series 21654, p. 92.

328. June 26th, 1758. Bouquet's Orderly Book. *Bouquet Papers*, Vol. II. p. 660.

329. Braddock to Robert Napier, Williamsburg, March 17th, 1755. *Pargellis*, p. 79.

330. May 2nd, 1755. *Seaman's Journal, Sargent*, p. 371.

331. *Munro*, p. 309.

332. *Knox*, Vol. I, p. 98.

333. July 21th, 1757. *Bouquet Papers*, Series 21631 & 21632, p. 42.

334. New York, December 27th, 1757. *Ibid.*, p. 155.

335. November, 1759. *Knox*, Vol. II, p. 291.

336. Crown Point, August 9th, 1759. *Commissary Wilson's Orderly Book*.

337. *Fit for Service*, p. 40.

338. *Mutiny Act*, 1758, p. 155.

339. Philo-Militum, and Richard Molesworth. *The case of the infantry in Ireland*, (1753), p. 13-14.

340. *Mutiny Act*, 1758, p. 178.

341. *Ibid.*, p. 156. See also *Bouquet Papers*, Series 21643, p. 28. Charlestown, March ?, 1758: *"...By the act of Parliament their Host is obliged for 4d stg. P. diem to provide them Breakfast, Dinner & Supper besides small Beer"*.

342. *Mutiny Act*, 1758, p. 160.

343. *Bouquet Papers*, Series 21631 & 21632, p. 42-43.

344. *Ibid.*, Series 21643, p. 29-30.

345. Charlestown, December 2nd, 1757. *Bouquet Papers*, Series 21643, p. 16-17.

346. *Knox*, Vol. II, p. 354.

347. September, 1753. *Wolfe in Scotland*, p. 298.

348. *"In every room occupied by Soldiers, pegs or nails should be drove into the driest and most convenient part of the wall, for the Arms , Accoutrements and Knapsacks, which must at all times be hung up in so regular and exact a manner, that every Man may in an instant, and without the least confusion, find his own, even in the dark; Nails should likewise be fixed for the *Hats , that they may be constantly hung up, when not in use; by which care, and placing them with the hind flaps"*. Cuthbertson, Chapter IX, Article XI.

349. *Bland*, 8th Edition, p. 225. See also *Knox*, Vol. II, p. 354. March, 1760.

350. *Ibid.*, p. 225.

351. *Cuthbertson*, Chapter XIV, Article XV.

352. *Bland*, 8th Edition, p. 225.

353. *Cuthbertson*, Chapter IX, Article XXIII.

354. *Knox*, Vol. II, p. 406.

355. September 30th, 1759. *Eddy*, p. 92.

356. *"The officers were allowed according to their Respective Rank Viz. To Field officers, each 3 rooms ready furnish'd. To Captains , each 2 Ditto, to Subalterns, each 1 Ditto"*. March, 1758. *Bouquet Papers*, Series 21643, p. 29.

357. *Bland*, 8th Edition, p. 178.

358. *Mutiny Act*, 1758, p. 160.

359. *Munro*, p. 317-318.

360. *Forbes*, p. 63.

361. *Knox*, Vol. II, p. 284.

362. Col. Henry Bouquets proposal for a winter expedition, 1759. *Bouquet Papers*, Series 21643, p. 220.

363. Montreal, December 6th, 1762. *Hervey*, p. 176.

364. December 12th, 1758. *Knox*, Vol, I, p. 285.

365. New York, March 5th, 1759. *Bouquet papers*, Series 21644, p. 76.

366. Major John Tulleken to Col. Henry Bouquet, Pittsburgh, March 1st, 1760. *Ibid.*, Series 21645, p. 44.

367. *Knox*, Vol. II, p. 305

368. November, 1759. *Knox*, Vol. I, p. 259.

369. December 29th, 1757. *Ibid.*, Vol. I, p. 133-134.

370. December 1759. *Ibid.*, Vol. I, p. 314.

371. The above quotes from *Knox*, Vol. II, December, 1759 to January 1760, p. 312-319

372. December, 1759. *Ibid.*, Vol. I, p. 316.

373. December, 1759. *Ibid.*, Vol. II, p. 294-295.

374. Wolfe to his mother, September 17th, 1757. *Wolfe Letters*, p. 326-327.

375. *Curtis*.

376. *Fit for Service*, p. 25.

377. Portsmouth, February 7th, 1758. *Wolfe Letters*, p. 357.

378. September 9th, 1757. *Todd*, p. 22-23.

379. *A soldier's journal*.

380. September 8th, 1757. *Todd*, p. 22.

381. September 18th, 1758. *Ibid.*, p.103.

382. *Curtis*, p. 23.

383. *Munro*, p. 325.

384. New York, May 17th, 1757. *Loudoun Papers*.

385. April 26th, 1759. *Eddy*, p. 19.

386. *Wolfe Letters*, p. 426.

387. August 17th, 1757. *Knox*, Vol. I, p. 53

388. *Knox*, Vol. I, p. 58

Grenadier's brass match case
(shown in black and white)
Length: 6.89"
Courtesy:
Parks Canada/Fortress of Louisbourg/
National Historic Site of Canada/
Image number: 79-147-7

389. *Wolfe Letters*, p. 426.

390. *Ibid.*

391. September 9th, 1757. *Todd*, p.23.

392. *Munro*, p. 330.

393. *Ibid.*

394. New York, May 17th, 1757. *Loudoun Papers*.

395. June 28th, 1757. *Knox*, Vol. I, p. 27.

396. Kielmansegge, Friedrich, graf von, *A diary of a journey to England in the years 1761-1762*. (London, New York: Longmans, Green, and co., 1902), p. 258-259.

397. *Ibid.*

398. The Disarming Act, 1746. Found in: *English Historical Documents*, Vol. 10, 1714-1783. David C. Douglas, D. B. Horn, Mary Ransome eds. (London: Eyre & Spottiswoode, 1957), p. 656-661.

399. Brander, Michael, *The Scottish Highlanders and their Regiments*. (New York: Barnes & Noble, 1996), p. 203-208.

400. June 4th, 1761. *Stewart's*.

401. September 21st, 1757. *Knox*, Vol. I, p. 73.

402. Scarlett, James D., *The Origins and Development of Military Tartans, A Re-Appraisal,* (Leigh-on-Sea: Partizan, 2003).

403. Henry Fox to Bland, November 7th, 1748. *Whitworth*, p. 131.

404. *Brander*, p. 29.

405. September 20th, 1761. *Stewart's*.

406. April 20th, 1761. *Ibid.*

See also *Ibid.* for August 6th, 1761: *"As the men are not yet provided with Cockades, returns also to be given in to the Qr.Mr. of the numbers wanted in each company, which are to be of black satine ribband allowing a yard and a quarter for each cockade"*,

and *Ibid.* for August 28th, 1761: *"...it requiring only one yard and half quarter of black Satine Riband inch broad for each cockade"*.

407. May 29th, 1761. *Stewart's*.

See also *Ibid.* for August 28th, 1761: *"As a great many of the Tifts in the mens bonnets are brown and not made according to the pattern which was shown at Montreal, they are therefore also to complete themselves immediately with proper tifts, made of the blackest bearskin that can be procured and not to exceed 5 inches in length which are to be fixed inclining towards the crown of the bonnets"*.

408. May 31st, 1761. *Stewart's*.

409. August 28th, 1761. *Ibid.*

410. September 9th, 1761. *Ibid.*

411. April 20th, 1760. *Ibid.*

412. *"...as its necessary also that the men be furnished with two white stocks of figured tape and one pair of scarlet tape for garters..."*. April 20th, 1760. *Stewart's*. See also *Ibid.* for September 9th, 1761.

413. New York, March 22nd, 1759. *Ibid.*

414. Bailey, De Witt, *British Military Smallarms in North America, 1755-1783*. (Bulletin of the American Society of Arms Collectors, #71, October 12-16, 1994).

415. Albany, May 5th, 1759. *Knox*, Vol. I, p. 459-460.

416. Return of swords in the Tower, 1756. *Cumberland papers, box 46. 150-151*. Found in *JSAHR*, Vol. XXVIII, No. 113. Rev. Percy Sumner Ed. (1950), p. 43.

417. April 16th, 1759. *Stewart's*.

418. Claude , Blair, Woosnam-Savage, Robert, *Scottish Firearms*, Historical Arms Series, No. 31. (Bloomfield, Ont.: Museum Restoration Service, 1995), p. 35.

419. May 18th, 1759. *Stewart's*.

420. May 2nd, 1761. *Ibid.*

421. October 31ˢᵗ, 1759. *Stewart's*.

422. November 13ᵗʰ, 1759. *Ibid.*

423. October 15ᵗʰ, 1761. *Ibid.*

424. April 30ᵗʰ, 1759. *Ibid.*

425. *"Each man to be dressed and accoutered conformable to Sir Jeffery Amherts orders of 1759 respecting the Light Infantry of Regiments"*. November 6ᵗʰ, 1761. *Stewart's*.

426. *Knox*, Vol. I, p. 74.

427. Wolfe to Lord George Sackville, Halifax, May 12ᵗʰ, 1758. *Wolfe Letters*, p. 363.

428. See *Todd*, part II.

429. June 10ᵗʰ, 1761. *Todd*, p. 144.

430. June 11ᵗʰ, 1761. *Ibid.*, p. 145. See also *Cuthbertson*, Chapter XXVII, Article I.

431. November 7ᵗʰ, 1761. *Todd*, p. 219.

432. June 11ᵗʰ, 1761. *Ibid.*, p. 145.

433. See *"The March to Finchley"* by William Hogarth (1697-1764). The Foundling Museum, London.

434. June 10ᵗʰ, 1761. *Todd*, p.144.

435. July 15ᵗʰ, 1761. *Ibid.*, p. 164.

436. Bland, Humphrey, *Treatise of Military Discipline*, 7ᵗʰ Edition. (London: 1753), p. 294.

437. June 17ᵗʰ, 1761. *Todd*, p. 149.

438. *1751 Royal Clothing Warrant*.

439. *A Soldier's Journal*.

440. June 7ᵗʰ, 1761. *Todd*, p. 143.

441. *A Soldier's Journal*.

442. *Bland*, 8ᵗʰ Edition, p. 294.

443. General Orders, January 3ʳᵈ, 1756. *Washington Manuscript*.

444. June 20ᵗʰ, 1755. *Orme's Journal, Sargent*, p. 339.

445. Halifax, July 28ᵗʰ, 1757. *Loudoun Papers*.

446. See *Hervey*, p. 76, 80, and 82.

447. *1751 Royal Clothing Warrant*.

448. *Chartrand*, p. 12.

449. *1751 Royal Clothing Warrant*.

450. *Chartrand*, p. 12.

451. Col. Henry Bouquet to Major William Walters, Fort Pitt, June 10ᵗʰ, 1761. *Bouquet Papers*, Series 21653, p. 61.

452. Found in Rickword, G. O., *The Buffs, 3ʳᵈ Regiment of Foot, Band concert, 1749. JSAHR*. Vol. XXXI, No. 128. (1953), p. 182.

453. May 24ᵗʰ, 1761. *Todd*, p. 136.

454. *Chartrand*, p. 12.

455. Waugh, W. T., *James Wolfe: Man and Soldier*. (New York: L. Carrier & co., 1928), p. 68.

456. March 27ᵗʰ, 1755. *Braddock's Orderly Book*, p. VIII.

457. Albany, May 5ᵗʰ, 1759. *Knox*, Vol. I, p. 459-460.

458. *JSAHR*, Vol. XXIII, No. 94, p. 82-83.

459. George Washington to Alexander Boyd, November 1ˢᵗ, 1755. *Washington Manuscript*.

460. April 6ᵗʰ, 1756. *Todd*, p. 14.

461. *Ibid.*

462. *The Cadet*, p. 107-108.

463. *Houlding*, p. 103.

464. Charteris, Evan, Sir, *William Augustus Duke of Cumberland and the Severn Years War*. (London: 1925), p. 83.

465. Found in *Lord Loudoun in North America*, p. 308.

466. *Guy*, p.40.

467. *Ibid.*, p. 36.

468. *Ibid.*, p. 137.

469. *Bland*, 8ᵗʰ Edition, p. 134.

470. October 5ᵗʰ, 1755. *Washington Manuscript*.

471. New York, April 9ᵗʰ, 1759. *Stewart's*.

472. *Chartrand*, p.16.

473. General orders given at Fort Edward, January 31ˢᵗ, 1760. *Stewart's*.

474. Governor Dinwiddie to JNO, Hanbury ESQ., March 12ᵗʰ, 1754. Dinwiddie, Robert, *The Official Records of Robert Dinwiddie, Lieutenant-Governor of the Colony of Virginia 1751-1758*. (Richmond: Virginia Historical Society, 1883-84).

475. The Cumberland Society was an anti-Jacobite society founded by the Duke of Cumberland and officers serving at the battle of Culloden. Every member who served in the military was required to wear their medal openly in combat. See Oughton, James Adolphus, *By dint of labour and perseverance: a journal recording two months in northern Germany*. Transcribed by Stephen Wood. (London: Society for Army Historical Research, 1997). The Blue and Orange society was a pro-Hanoverian society, formed by officers of the 4ᵗʰ Regiment around 1730.

476. *Bland*, 8ᵗʰ Edition, p. 289.

477. October 28ᵗʰ, 1761. *Todd*, p. 215.

478. September 1ˢᵗ, 1757. *Knox*, Vol. I, p. 64.

479. November, 1759. *Ibid.*, Vol. II, p. 291.

480. April 27ᵗʰ, 1762. Brigade Order Books. *Hervey*, p. 162.

481. October 27ᵗʰ, 1761. *Todd*, p. 215.

482. O'Conor, Norreys, J., *A Servant of the Crown in England and in North America, 1756-1761. Based upon the papers of John Appy, secretary and Judge Advocate of his Majesty's forces*. (New York: D. Appleton-Century Co., 1938), p. 173-227.

483. *Wolfe in Scotland*, p. 294.

484. May 11ᵗʰ, 1758. *Moneypenny*.

485. New York, January 16ᵗʰ, 1759. *Amherst and the Conquest of Canada*, p. 15.

486. March 27ᵗʰ, 1755. *Braddock's Orderly Books*, p. VIII.

487. Camp near Lake George, July 18th, 1758. *Journal of David Waterbury*, Collection of the Fort Ticonderoga Museum.

488. May, 1759. *Knox*, Vol. I, p. 350.

489. *Ibid.* Vol. I, p. 476.

490. *Bland*, 8th Edition, p. 134.

491. Wolfe to Hugh Lord, Date unknown. *Wolfe Letters*, p. 298.

See also *Stewart's* for May 26th, 1761: *"It is Col. Grants orders that the officers shall provide themselves each, with a copy of the Dukes Regulations for the Firings as practiced in the year 1757, an extract of which they can have from the Regimental book, and it is expected that they will make themselves masters of the same"*.

492. June 22nd, 1758. *Knox*, Vol. I, p. 181.

493. *Guy*, p.56-57.

494. Camp at Alexandria, Virginia, March 31st, 1755. *Halkett's Orderly Book, Sargent*, p. 73.

495. Camp at Reas Town, June 26th, 1758. Bouquet Orderly Book. *Bouquet Papers*, Vol. II, p. 660.

496. *Guy*, p. 98.

497. May 21st, 1759, *Davenport*.

498. May 6th, 1755. *Sargent*, p. 371.

499. Dublin, February 2nd, 1742. *Bagshawe*, p. 39-40.

500. *Appy*, p. 173-227.

501. *Bouquet Papers*, Series 21631 & 21632, p.143-144, and *Loudoun's Papers*, July, 1757. These rates probably changed depending on available food supplies. According to Loudoun, in 1757 a Lieutenant Colonel received four rations per day.

502. Col. Henry Bouquet to Ensign Lachlan McIntosh, February 16th, 1758. *Bouquet Papers*, Series 21631 & 21632, p. 143-144.

503. February 15th, 1758. *Knox*, Vol. I, p. 139.

504. Lieutenant-Colonel Samuel Bagshawe's account of his income and expenditure. *Guy*, p. 98.

505. *Bouquet*, Vol. II, p. 352-253.

506. Wolfe to his mother, March 25th, 1749. *Wolfe Letters*, p. 90-91.

507. July 20th, 1758. *Moneypenny*.

508. August 26th, 1759. *Wolfe's General Orders*.

509. March 18th, 1755. *Seaman's Journal*, found in *Sargent*, p. 377.

510. Wolfe to Lord George Sackville, May 24th, 1758. *Wolfe Letters*, p. 369.

511. April 8th, 1755. *Halkett's Orderly Book, Hamilton*, p. 77.

512. Major Burd's proposal for the better securing the Province of Pennsylvania, 1757. *Pennsylvania Archives*, Vol. III, p. 99-104.

513. *Grant*, Vol. II, p. 21-22.

514. *Chartrand*, p. 13.

515. *Hawks*, p. 19-20.

516. Rogers, H. C. B., *The British Army of the Eighteenth Century*. (New York: 1977).

517. *WO 30/13A.*

518. *JSAHR*, Vol. XXXVI, No. 146. (1958), p. 76-77.

519. *Knox*, Vol. I, p. 207.

520. November 22nd - 23rd, 1759. *Ibid.*, Vol. I, p. 281.

521. May, 1759. *Ibid.* Vol. I, p. 352-353.

522. Crown Point, November 22nd, 1759. *Stewart's*.

523. December, 1759. *Knox*, Vol. II, p. 295.

524. *"Those that have not cartouche boxes must break open their cartridges and put their powder into horns"*. May 31st, 1759. *Hawks*, p. 7.

525. December, 1759. *Knox*, Vol. II, p. 295.

526. Major General Amherst to Colonel Arthur Morris, New York, April 19th, 1759. *Amherst and the Conquest of Canada*, p. 48.

527. February, 1760. *Knox*, Vol. II, p. 334.

528. *Amherst and the Conquest of Canada*, p. 74.

529. Amherst to Colonel Haldimand, Camp at Fort Levis, August 23rd, 1760. *Ibid.*, p. 213.

530. Instructions for the Reduction of the 42nd Regiment, August 7th, 1763. *Bouquet Papers*, Series 21653, p. 211-212.

531. Royal Warrant, George Rex, St. James, May 18th 1763. *Bouquet Papers*, Series 21634, p. 167-169.

532. Instructions for the Reduction of the 42nd Regiment, August 7th, 1763. *Bouquet Papers*, Series 21653, p. 211-212.

533. Bartlett, Thomas, Jeffery, Keith, *A Military History of Ireland*. (Cambridge: 1996). p. 213.

534. Col. Henry Bouquet to General Napier, Charlestown, South Carolina, July 13th, 1757. *Bouquet Papers*, Series 21631 & 21632, p.29.

535. *Ipswich Journal Newspaper*, March 31st, 1759.

536. *Kielmansegge*, p. 275-276.

537. *Ibid.*

538. *Ibid.*

539. Parkyn, Major H.G., *Shoulder-Belt Plates and Buttons*. (Aldershot, Eng: Gale & Polden, 1956), p. 3.

Bibliography

War Office Series:

WO 26/21, Entry books of warrants, regulations and precedents, 1746-1751.

WO 30/13a, Clothing Register of Correspondence, 1751-1794.

Manuscripts:

Loudoun, John Campbell, Earl of. *Lord Loudoun Papers*. Huntington Library. San Marino, CA.

Papers:

Redmon, Barton J. *Grand and Petit Sutlers of the British Army during the era of the Seven Years War 1755-1765*.

Periodicals:

Bulletin of the American Society of Arms Collectors.

    #71, October 12-16, 1994.

Bulletin of the Fort Ticonderoga Museum.

    Vol. XII, No. 5-6.

    Vol. XIII, No. 1.

Journal of The Company of Military Historians.

    Vol. XXXV, No. 1.

Journal of The Society for Army Historical Research.

    Vol. XXIII, No. 94.

    Vol. XXVI. No. 107.

    Vol. XXVII, No. 112.

    Vol. XXVIII, No. 113.

    Vol. XXXI, No. 128.

    Vol. XXXVI, No. 146.

    Vol. LXIV, No. 257.

Military Illustrated Magazine.

    #81.

Primary Sources:

Amherst, Jeffery. *The journal of Jeffery Amherst, recording the military career of General Amherst in America from 1758 to 1763*. J. C. Webster, ed. Chicago: University of Chicago Press, 1931. *Amherst and the Conquest of Canada, Selected Papers from the Correspondence of Major-General Jeffery Amherst while Commander-in-Chief in North America from September 1758 to December 1760*. Richard Middleton ed. Army Records Society, Vol. 20. Sutton Publishing, LTD., 2003. Wilson, & O'Callaghan, E. B. *Commissary Wilson's orderly book: expedition of the British and provincial army, under Maj. Gen. Jeffrey Amherst, against Ticonderoga and Crown Point, 1759*. Albany: J. Munsell, 1857.

Andrews, Frank De Witte. *Connecticut soldiers in the French and Indian war; bills, receipts and documents printed from the original manuscripts*. Vineland, New Jersey: Private, 1925.

Bagshawe, Samuel, Guy, Alan J. *Colonel Bagshawe and the Army of George II, 1731-1762*. London: Bodley Head for the Army Records Society, 1990.

Beckles, Willson. *The Life and Letters of James Wolfe*. London: W. Heinemann, 1909.

Bland, Humphrey. *A treatise of military discipline : in which is laid down and explained the duty of the officer and soldier, through the several branches of the service*, 7th Edition. London: 1753. 8th Edition. London: 1759.

Bouquet, Henry. *Papers of Col. Henry Bouquet*. Harrisburg: Pennsylvania historical commission, 1940.

Bouquet, Henry, K.S. Stevens, ed. *The Papers of Henry Bouquet*, Vol. II. *The Forbes Expedition*. Harrisburg: Pennsylvania Historical Commission, 1951.

Braddock, Edward. *Major General Edward Braddock's Orderly Books, from February 26 to June 17, 1755, From the Originals, in the Congressional Library*. Cumberland, MD: 1878.

The Cadet, A Military Treatise, 2nd Edition. anon. London: 1762.

Cumberland, William Augustus. *Exercise for the Foot, with the differences to be observed in the Dragoon Exercise 1757. By Order Of H.R.H. Prince William Augustus Duke of Cumberland*. Reprinted as Historical Arms Series, No. 42. Bloomfield, Ont: Museum Restoration Service, 2004.

Cuthbertson, Bennet. *A system for the complete interior management and oeconomy of a battalion of infantry*. Dublin: 1768. *The Compleat Cuthbertson A Modern Edition Combining the Several Editions*. Mark Tully, Don Hagist, eds. Ballindalloch Press, 2000.

Dalrymple, Campbell. *A military essay; containing reflections on the raising, arming, cloathing, and discipline of the British infantry and Cavalry, with proposals for the improvement of the same*. London, D. Wilson, 1761.

Darlington, Mary C. *Fort Pitt and Letters from the Frontier*. Pittsburgh: J.R. Weldin & Co., 1892.

Dinwiddie, Robert. *The Official Records of Robert Dinwiddie, Lieutenant-Governor of the Colony of Virginia 1751-1758*. Richmond, Virginia: The Society, 1883-84.

Douglas, David C. Horn D. B., Ransome, Mary, eds. *English Historical Documents*, Vol. 10, 1714-1783. London: Eyre & Spottiswoode, 1957.

Eddy, Jonathan. *Fragment and orderly book by Capt. Jonathan Eddy, 1755-1759*. Clara A. Avery ed. Boston: T.O. Metcalf Co., 1927.

Findlay, J.T. *Wolfe in Scotland in the '45 and from 1749 to 1753*. London: Longmans, Green and co., 1928.

Fitzpatrick, John C. ed. *The Writings of Washington from the Original Manuscript Sources, 1745-1799*. Washington: U. S. Govt. print. off. 1931-44.

Forbes, John. *Letters of General John Forbes relating to the expedition against Fort Duquesne in 1758 compiled from books in the Carnegie Library of Pittsburgh for the Allegheny County Committee, Pennsylvania Society of the Colonial Dames of America*. Stewart, Irene, ed. Pittsburgh: Allegheny County Committee, 1927.

Foster, Henry. *The Journal of Henry Foster, of Sturbridge Massachusetts, during the French and Indian War, May 27 – October 27, 1758*.

Grant, Anne MacVicar. *Memoirs of an American lady: with sketches of manners and scenery in America as they existed previous to the revolution*. New York: G. Appleton, 1846.

Great Britain. *An act for punishing Mutiny and Desertion; and for the better Payment of the Army and their Quarters*. London: 1758.

Gridley, Luke. *Luke Gridley's Diary of 1757 while in the service in the French and Indian War*. Connecticut: Acorn Club of Connecticut publications, 1907.

Guy, Alan J. *Oeconomy and discipline, officership and administration in the British army, 1714-63*. Manchester: Manchester University Press, 1985.

Hamilton, Charles. *Braddock's defeat; the journal of Captain Robert Cholmley's batman, the journal of a British officer [and] Halkett's orderly book*. Norman: University of Oklahoma Press: 1959.

Hamilton, Stanislaus, M. ed. *Letters to Washington and Accompanying Papers*. Cambridge: The Society of the Colonial Dames of American, 1898-1902. Library of Congress online: http://memory.loc.gov/ammem/gwhtml/gwhome.html.

Hawks, John. *Orderly book and journal of Major John Hawks on the Ticonderoga-Crown Point campaign, under General Jeffrey Amherst, 1759-1760*. New York: Society of Colonial Wars in the State of New York, 1911.

Hervey, William. *Journals of Hon. William Hervey, in North America and Europe, From 1755-1814; with Order Books at Montreal 1760-1763. With Memoir and Notes*. Bury St. Edmund's: Paul & Mathew, 1906.

Kielmansegge, Friedrich, graf von. *A diary of a journey to England in the years 1761-1762*. London, New York: Longmans, Green, and co., 1902.

Kirk, Robert. *The Memoirs and Adventures of Robert Kirk, Late of the Royal Highland Regiment, Written by himself*. Limerick: printed by J. Ferrar, 1770.

Knox, John. *An historical journal of the campaigns in North America for the years 1757, 1758, 1759, and 1760*, Vol. I-II. Freeport, N.Y., Books for Libraries Press, 1970.

Lyman, Phineas. *General orders of 1757: issued by the Earl of Loudoun and Phineas Lyman in the campaign against the French*. New York: Dodd, Mead, 1899.

Munro, Donald, M.D. *An Account of the Diseases which were most frequent in the British Military Hospitals in Germany, from January 1761 to the return of the Troops to England in March 1763*. London: Printed for A. Millar, D. Wilson, T. Durham, and T. Payne, 1764.

O'Conor, Norreys, J. *A Servant of the Crown in England and in North America, 1756-1761. Based upon the papers of John Appy, secretary and Judge Advocate of his Majesty's forces*. New York: D. Appleton-Century Co., 1938.

Oughton, James Adolphus. *By dint of labour and perseverance: a journal recording two months in northern Germany*. Transcribed by Stephen Wood. London: Society for Army Historical Research, 1997.

Pargellis, Stanley M. *Lord Loudoun in North America*. Hamden, Connecticut: Archon Books, 1968. *Military Affairs in North America 1748-65: Selected Documents from the Cumberland Papers in Windsor Castle*. Hamden, Connecticut: Archon Books, 1969.

Pennsylvania Archives, 2nd Series, Vol. II-III. Harrisburg: J. Severns & Co.,1876

Perry, David. *Recollections of an old soldier: the life of Captain David Perry, a soldier of the French and Revolutionary wars*. Windsor, Vermont: Republican & Yeoman Printing Office, 1822.

Philo-Militum, and Richard Molesworth. *The case of the infantry in Ireland humbly addressed to the Right Honourable Richard, Lord Viscount Molesworth... and to the general officers on the establishment in Ireland*. 1753.

Pitt, William, Earl of Chatham, William Stanhope Taylor, and John Henry Pringle. *Correspondence of William Pitt, Earl of Chatham*, Vol. I. London: J. Murray, 1838.

Pouchot, Pierre. *Memoir upon the late war in North America, between the French and English, 1755-60*. Vol. I. Franklin B. Hough, ed. Roxbury, Massachusetts: Printed for W.E. Woodward, 1866.

Shirley, William, and Charles Henry Lincoln. *Correspondence of William Shirley, governor of Massachusetts and military commander in America, 1731-1760*. New York: Macmillan Co. 1912.

Simes, Thomas. *The Military Guide for Young Officers*. London: 1776.

Simmons, R.C., Thomas, P.D.G. eds. *Proceedings and Debates of the British Parliament Respecting North America 1754-1783*, Vol. I. Millwood, New York: Kraus International Publications, 1982.

A Soldier's journal, containing a particular description of the several descents on the coast of France last war with an entertaining account of the islands of Guadaloupe, Dominique, &c. and also of the isles of Wight and Jersey. To which are annexed, Observations on the present state of the army of Great Britain. London: Printed for E. and C. Dilly, 1770.

Stewart, Captain James. *Order Book of the Royal Highland Regiment 1759-1761*. Wm. B. Wilson, ed. Perth: Black Watch Museum, 1947.

Timberlake, Henry, Williams, Samuel Cole. *Memoirs, 1756-1765*. Merietta, GA: Continental Books Co., 1948.

Todd, William. *The Journal of Corporal Todd 1745-1762*. Andrew Cormack, Alan Jones, ed. Publications of the Army Records Society, Vol. 18, 2001.

Townshend, Charles Vere Ferrers, Sir. *The military life of Field-Marshal George first Marquess Townshend, 1724-1807, who took part in the battles of Dettingen 1743, Fontenoy 1745, Culloden 1746, Laffeldt 1747, & in the capture of Quebec 1759*. London: J. Murray, 1901.

Washington, George. *Letters to Washington and Accompanying Papers, published by the Society of the Colonial Dames of America*. Stanislaus Murray Hamilton, ed. Boston: Houghton, Mifflin and Co., 1898.

Willard, Abijah. *Journal of Abijah Willard of Lancaster, Mass., an officer in the expedition which captured Fort Beauséjour in 1755*. J.C. Webster, ed. St. John, N. B., 1930.

Williams, Edward. *The Orderly Book of Colonel Henry Bouquet's Expedition against the Ohio Indians, 1764*. Philadelphia: 1765.

Wolfe, James. *General orders in Major Wolfe's Army before Quebec. The orders cover the period commencing Louisbourg, 16th May 1759 during the expedition up the river St. Lawrence ending at the camp before Quebec, Tuesday, 18th Sept. 1759, after Wolfe's death*. Toronto: Canadian House, 1967. *Wolfe's Instructions for Young Officers*. London: Printed for J. Millan, 1778.

Secondary Sources:

Ahearn, Bill. *Muskets of the Revolutionary War and French & Indian War*. Rhode Island: Andrew Mowbray, 2005.

Bailey, De Witt. *Pattern Dates for British Ordnance Small Arms, 1718-1783*. Gettysburg: Thomas Publications, 1997.

Bartlett, Thomas, Jeffery, Keith. *A Military History of Ireland.* Cambridge: Cambridge University Press, 1996.

Blackmoore, Howard L. *British Military Firearms 1650-1850.* Mechanicsburg, PA.: Stackpole Books, 1994.

Brander, Michael. *The Scottish Highlanders and their Regiments.* New York: Barnes and Noble, 1996.

Charteris, Evan, Sir. *William Augustus Duke of Cumberland and the Severn Years War.* London: Hutchinson & co., 1925.

Chenciner, Robert. *Madder Red: a history of luxury and trade: plant dyes and pigments in world commerce and art.* Richmond: Curzon, 2000.

Claude, Blair, Woosnam-Savage, Robert. *Scottish Firearms.* Historical Arms Series, No. 31. Bloomfield, Ont.: Museum Restoration Service, 1995.

Clode, Charles M. *The Military Forces of the Crown: their administration and government.* London: 1869.

Crump, W. B., Joseph Rogerson, Benjamin Gott. *Leeds Woollen Industry 1780–1868.* Leeds: Thoresby Society, 1931.

Curtis, Edward E. *The Organization of the British Army in the American Revolution.* London: H. Milford, Oxford University Press, 1926.

Darling, Anthony D. *Red Coat and Brown Bess.* Historical Arms Series No. 12. New York: Museum Restoration Service, 1971.

Fielding, Henry. *The History of Tom Jones, a Foundling.* London: 1749.

Fortescue, J.W. *History of the British Army,* Vol. II. London: Macmillan, 1910-1930.

Goldstein, Erik. *18th Century Weapons of the Royal Welsh Fuziliers at Flixton Hall.* Gettysburg: Thomas Publications, 2002.

Houlding, J.A. *Fit For Service, The Training of the British Army, 1715–1795.* Oxford: Oxford University Press, 1981.

Lawson, Cecil C.P. *A history of the uniforms of the British Army.* London: P. Davies, 1940-1967.

Parkyn, Major H.G. *Shoulder-Belt Plates and Buttons.* Aldershot, Eng: Gale & Polden, 1956.

Rogers, H. C. B. *The British Army of the Eighteenth Century.* New York: Hippocrene Books, 1977.

Scarlett, James D. *The Origins and Development of Military Tartans, A Re-Appraisal.* Leigh-on-Sea: Partizan, 2003.

Stewart, Richard W. *The English Ordnance Office, A Case Study in Bureaucracy, 1585-1625.* Rochester, Royal Historical Society, Boydell Press: 1996.

Tann, Jennifer. *Gloucestershire Woollen Mills: industrial archaeology, The Industrial Archaeology of the British Isles.* Newton Abbot, Devon: David & Charles, 1967.

Waugh, W. T. *James Wolfe: Man and Soldier.* Montreal, New York: L. Carrier & co., 1928.

West, Jenny. *Gunpowder, Government, and War in the mid-18th century.* Rochester: Boydell Press, 1991.

Whitworth, Rex. *William Augustus, Duke of Cumberland, A Life.* London: Leo Cooper, 1992.

Winthrop, Sargent, ed. *The history of an expedition against Fort Du Quesne, in 1755, under Major-General Edward Braddock.* Philadelphia: Historical Society of Pennsylvania, 1855.

Photo by Christopher Cusick

Ryan Gale grew up in the north woods of Minnesota along the shore of Lake Superior, an area surrounded by history. Coming from a family with a long military heritage his fascination with military history developed at an early age. His interest in British history began after discovering that his forefather emigrated from England in the early 1800s. It didn't take long for his interests in military and British history to combine into one passion.

In the summer of 2002 Ryan graduated from college with a degree in graphic art and began a career as an artist and photographer, designing and writing history related websites and books. Besides being the author of this book, he also did the layout, design, and much of the photography. Ryan is an avid French & Indian War and Revolutionary War re-enactor, portraying British soldiers from the 42nd Royal Highland Regiment circa. 1759, and 55th Regiment circa. 1776. In 2003 he resurrected the 44th Regiment to celebrate the 250th anniversary of the French & Indian War. The regiment continues to flourish with members throughout the United States, Canada, and England. Ryan spends much of his free time studying history and creating historical artwork.